SCHOLASTIC

INTERACTIVE
Science Wheels

by Donald M. Silver and Patricia J. Wynne

NEW YORK ● TORONTO ● LONDON ● AUCKLAND ● SYDNEY
MEXICO CITY ● NEW DELHI ● HONG KONG ● BUENOS AIRES

Teaching Resources

For Mary Cardillo Utter,

With heart and mind

—DMS

For all of my editors at Scholastic

who care so much about children's science books

—PJW

Editor: Maria L. Chang
Designer: Kathy Massaro

ISBN: 978-0-439-32334-5
Copyright © 2013 by Donald M. Silver and Patricia J. Wynne
All rights reserved.
Printed in the U.S.A.

1 2 3 4 5 6 7 8 9 10   40   20 19 18 17 16 15 14 13

Contents

Introduction

The wheel is presumably humankind's most important invention. Almost every machine we build today includes at least one kind of wheel or another. In this book, we take advantage of the wheel's features to teach equally important science concepts. For young students, interactive wheels provide a simple yet effective way of representing recurring patterns in nature. Such recurring patterns include cycles, such as the seasons, the water cycle, the rock cycle, the phases of the moon, and the life cycles of plants and animals. Wheels can also be useful for classifying animals, rocks, and clouds, as well as identifying parts of plants, simple machines, and objects in the night sky.

This book presents different kinds of wheels. Each wheel is designed to draw students into the cycle, classification, or identification being described. Unlike most wheels that consist of two circles joined together with a paper fastener, just about all of the wheels in this book are shaped to the subject matter. For example, the wheel detailing the life cycle of a frog is in the shape of a frog sitting on a lily pad; the wheel classifying birds is in the shape of a pelican.

The wheels are easy to make and easy to read. Children will get a sense of accomplishment from creating and coloring their own wheels. Each wheel contains simple language and concepts as well as engaging pictures that will help children build skills and confidence as readers. From watching how a caterpillar becomes a butterfly to learning what simple machines do, children will be delighted by what their wheels look like and what they learn from them.

What's Inside

Interactive Science Wheels covers a range of topics in life science, earth science, and physical science. The wheels can be used in any order. Within each chapter are lessons that feature the following sections:

❄ **Science Corner:** A summary of the science background information you need to teach the lesson

❄ **Materials:** A short list of things students need to create the wheel

❄ **Making the Wheel:** Easy step-by-step instructions for assembling the wheel

✳ **Teaching With the Wheel:** A quick mini-lesson for introducing the science concept, plus text-based discussion questions

✳ **More to Do:** An engaging activity designed to extend learning

✳ **Resources:** Related books and websites for students and teachers

✳ **Reproducible Pages:** Ready-to-photocopy patterns for each wheel to be distributed to students

Helpful Hints

As with any new instructional material, it is always a good idea to make the wheels yourself before introducing them to your class. This way, you can anticipate any questions that may arise and be ready to help children as needed. Keep in mind the following tips for creating the wheels:

✳ The thickest solid lines on the reproducible pages are CUT lines.

✳ All of the wheels have grayed-out "windows" that require cutting out. An easy way to cut them is to use the "pinch method": Use your thumb and forefinger to fold the paper near one line and, taking your scissors, snip an opening. Then insert the scissors through the opening to easily cut open the window.

✳ If possible, enlarge the pattern pages to make the wheels easier for children to assemble.

✳ Encourage children to take their wheels home and share them with their families. You may also want to put additional copies and extra materials in a learning center so children can make and read the wheels on their own.

We hope that you and your students get as much fun and excitement out of these unique wheels as we had in creating them. Enjoy!

Science Standards

The following standards were taken from McREL (Mid-continent Research for Education and Learning), a nationally recognized, nonprofit organization, which has compiled and evaluated national and state standards for science and other content areas. For more information, visit: http://www.mcrel.org/standards-benchmarks/.

Standard 1. Understands atmospheric processes and the water cycle.

✳ Knows that short-term weather conditions can change daily, and weather patterns change over the seasons.

✳ Knows that water can be a liquid or a solid and can be made to change from one form to the other, but the amount of water stays the same.

✳ Knows that water exists in the air in different forms and changes from one form to another through various processes.

✳ Knows that the Sun provides the light and heat necessary to maintain the temperature of the Earth.

✳ Knows that air is a substance that surrounds us, takes up space, and moves around us as wind.

Standard 2. Understands Earth's composition and structure.

✳ Knows that Earth materials consist of solid rocks, soils, liquid water, and the gases in the atmosphere.

✳ Knows that rocks come in many different shapes and sizes.

✳ Knows how features on the Earth's surface are constantly changed by a combination of slow and rapid processes.

✳ Knows that rock is composed of different combinations of materials.

Standard 3. Understands the composition and structure of the universe and the Earth's place in it.

✳ Knows the basic patterns of the Sun and Moon.

✳ Knows that the stars are innumerable, unevenly dispersed, and of unequal brightness.

✳ Knows that the Earth is one of several planets that orbit the Sun and that the Moon orbits the Earth.

✳ Knows that planets look like stars, but over time they appear to wander among the constellations.

✳ Knows that astronomical objects in space are massive in size and are separated from one another by vast distances.

✳ Knows that telescopes magnify distant objects in the sky and dramatically increase the number of stars we can see.

Standard 4. Understands the principles of heredity and related concepts.

✳ Knows that plants and animals closely resemble their parents.

✳ Knows that many characteristics of plants and animals are inherited from its parents, and other characteristics result from an individual's interactions with the environment.

Standard 5. Understands the structure and function of cells and organisms.

✳ Knows the basic needs of plants and animals.

✳ Knows that plants and animals have features that help them live in different environments.

✳ Knows that plants and animals progress through life cycles of birth, growth and development, reproduction, and death; the details of these life cycles are different for different organisms.

✳ Knows that living organisms have distinct structures and body systems that serve specific functions in growth, survival, and reproduction.

Standard 6. Understands relationships among organisms and their physical environment.

✳ Knows that plants and animals need certain resources for energy and growth.

✳ Knows that living things are found almost everywhere in the world and that distinct environments support the life of different types of plants and animals.

✳ Knows the organization of simple food chains and food webs.

Standard 7. Understands biological evolution and the diversity of life.

✳ Knows that there are similarities and differences in the appearance and behavior of plants and animals.

✳ Knows different ways in which living things can be grouped and purposes of different groupings.

What Are Mammals?

**Meet the mammals—
furry, warm-blooded creatures,
large and small!**

Science Corner

Mammals are *vertebrates*—animals with backbones. The backbone is part of the skeleton, which supports the body, helps give it shape, and protects delicate organs such as the heart, brain, and lungs. Mammals breathe air through lungs. They are the only animals that grow hair or fur, which helps keep them warm. Mammals make their own body heat. Because of this, they can be active at night and in cold weather. Mammals are also the only animals with sweat glands in their skin. When most mammals overheat, they sweat to cool down.

Most mammals give birth to live babies. The only exceptions are the duck-billed platypus and the echidna, which lay eggs. Once a baby mammal is born, its mother produces milk to feed it. Only mammals have mammary glands able to produce milk. Mammal parents care for and protect their young until they are old enough to survive on their own. The parents teach their young how to find food and avoid danger.

Mammals live all over the world—from the frigid polar regions to the hottest deserts, in tropical rain forests, grasslands, caves, and even in oceans. There are about 4,200 kinds of mammals, including dogs, cats, horses, lions, mice, beavers, bats, dolphins, and human beings. Mammals boast the largest and most powerful land animal (elephant), the tallest (giraffe), and the fastest (cheetah). The largest of all animals is also a mammal—the blue whale, measuring 100 feet (30 m) long and weighing more than 150 tons (135,000 kg).

Materials

* reproducible pages 9 and 10
* scissors
* paper fastener
* colored pencils, crayons, or markers (optional)

More To Do

Mammal Chart

Challenge students to research the following mammals: duck-billed platypus, kangaroo, giant anteater, horseshoe bat, chipmunk, sloth, elephant, rabbit, harp seal, polar bear, zebra, aye-aye. Have them find out where these animals live, what they eat, and what other mammals are related to them. Make a chart of the different groups of mammals. Invite students to draw pictures of their mammals for the chart.

Resources

***Super Swimmers: Whales, Dolphins, and Other Mammals of the Sea* by Caroline Arnold (Charlesbridge, 2007)**

Beautifully illustrated whales, dolphins, and other sea mammals will draw young readers into the world of sea mammals.

***Lions* by Jill Anderson (Cooper Square, 2006)**

Simple text and full-color photos offer a glimpse into the life of a lion family.

http://naturemapping foundation.org/natmap/ facts/mammals.html

Click on a photo or an animal name to find out cool facts about the mammal.

Making the Wheel

1 Photocopy pages 9 and 10. Color, if desired.

2 Cut out the raccoon and the wheel along the thick outer lines.

3 Cut open the CUT OUT window and the small triangular notch on the raccoon along the thick solid lines.

4 Place the raccoon on top of the wheel. Push the paper fastener through the centers of both pieces to join them, as shown.

Teaching With the Wheel

Ask students if they have a pet dog, cat, hamster, gerbil, guinea pig, or mouse. Explain that such pets are mammals. Invite students to describe their pets. Ask: *How big are they? What covers their body? What do they like to eat?* Encourage students to bring in and share photos of their pets. To learn more about mammals and where they live, invite students to color, make, and read their wheels. Then check for understanding by asking them these questions:

1 What are mammals? (*Mammals are the only animals that grow hair or fur. They make their own body heat to keep warm. They breathe air through lungs.*)

2 What do mammals feed their babies? (*Milk they make*)

3 Name some animals that live in the grasslands [or other habitat]. (*Giraffe, bison, lion*)

What Are Mammals?

Mammals are the only animals that grow hair or fur. They make their own body heat to keep warm. They breathe air through lungs. Mammals live everywhere on earth.

Mammals make milk to feed their babies. They take care of their young.

CUT OUT

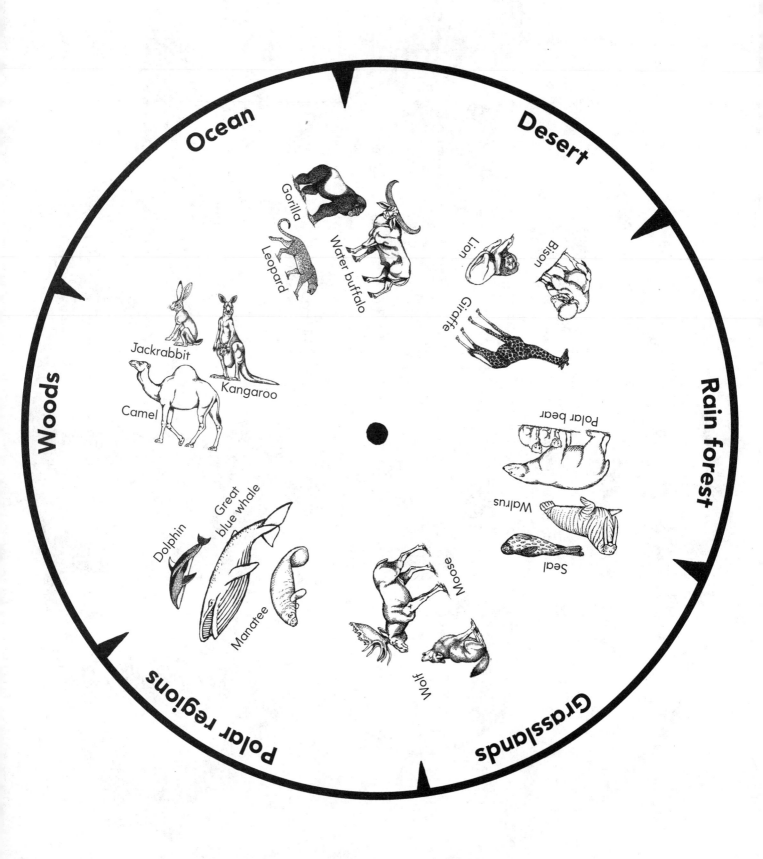

What Are Birds?

Most feathered friends can fly, but a few prefer to swim. Learn more about birds with this wheel.

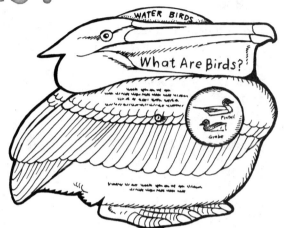

Science Corner

There are more than 8,600 kinds of birds in the world. The largest are ostriches that can grow up to 8 feet (2.4 m) tall; the smallest are hummingbirds, which are about 2 inches (5 cm) long. The biggest group of birds is perching birds, such as robins and sparrows. Perching birds have four toes on each foot—three that point forward and one that points backward. When perching birds land on a branch and bend their legs, their toes lock tightly in place so the birds don't fall off.

Birds are vertebrates (animals with backbones) and the only animals with feathers. Like mammals, birds can make their own body heat. On cold days, birds fluff their feathers to stop body heat from escaping. On hot days, they spread their feathers to keep from overheating. In addition to protecting a bird's body, feathers also help birds fly. Most birds have lightweight bodies and powerful flying muscles. A bird flies by beating its wings up and down. Some birds can fly at a speed of 100 miles per hour (160 km per hour), and some can fly thousands of miles without stopping. Some birds, such as ostriches and penguins, cannot fly.

While penguins and some other birds can swim, they cannot live underwater because they breathe air through lungs. Birds live everywhere on land. They build nests out of leaves, twigs, and mud where predators cannot easily find or reach them. They line the nests with feathers or other soft material to protect their eggs. Most birds care for their young until the young can fly and find food for themselves.

Birds have strong, lightweight beaks adapted for different kinds of food. Predatory hawks have hooked beaks for tearing flesh; diving birds have long, pointed beaks for spearing and holding fish; and insect-eating birds have sharp, pointed beaks.

Materials

❄ reproducible pages 13 and 14

❄ scissors

❄ paper fastener

❄ colored pencils, crayons, or markers (optional)

More To Do

Bird Book

Invite students to select one of the birds on their bird wheel and find out more about it. Where does the bird live? What does it eat? What kind of nest does it build? How many eggs does it lay? Have students draw pictures of their bird and write a short description of it based on their research. Be sure to include the pelican that makes up the cover of the wheel. Staple all of the students' work together to create a class bird book.

Resources

Watching Water Birds
by Jim Aronsky (National Geographic Children's Books, 2002)

Beautiful paintings capture water birds in action as they dive, swim, and fly.

City Hawk: The Story of Pale Male by Meghan McCarthy (Simon & Schuster, 2007)

Follow the story of two red-tailed hawks who built a nest and raised two chicks on an apartment building in Manhattan.

http://www.enature.com/ birding/audio.asp

Click on the bird names to learn more about them and hear their calls.

Making the Wheel

1 Photocopy pages 13 and 14. Color, if desired.

2 Cut out the pelican and the wheel along the thick outer lines.

3 Cut open the CUT OUT window and the small triangular notch on the pelican along the thick solid lines.

4 Place the pelican on top of the wheel. Push the paper fastener through the centers of both pieces to join them, as shown.

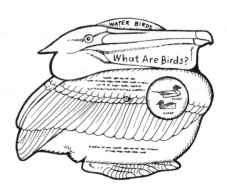

Teaching With the Wheel

Ask students: *What birds have you recently seen near your home, the school, or the park?* Have them describe the birds and what the birds were doing. Ask students if they remember seeing birds at the beach, in the mountains, or in the woods. How are those birds alike or different from the birds they see around their city or town?

To learn more about different kinds of birds, invite students to color, make, and read their wheels. Then check for understanding by asking them these questions:

1 What are birds? (*Birds are the only animals with feathers. Like mammals, they make their own body heat.*)

2 How do birds fly? (*Birds beat their wings up and down to fly.*)

3 Can all birds fly? (*All birds have feathers and wings, but not all birds can fly.*)

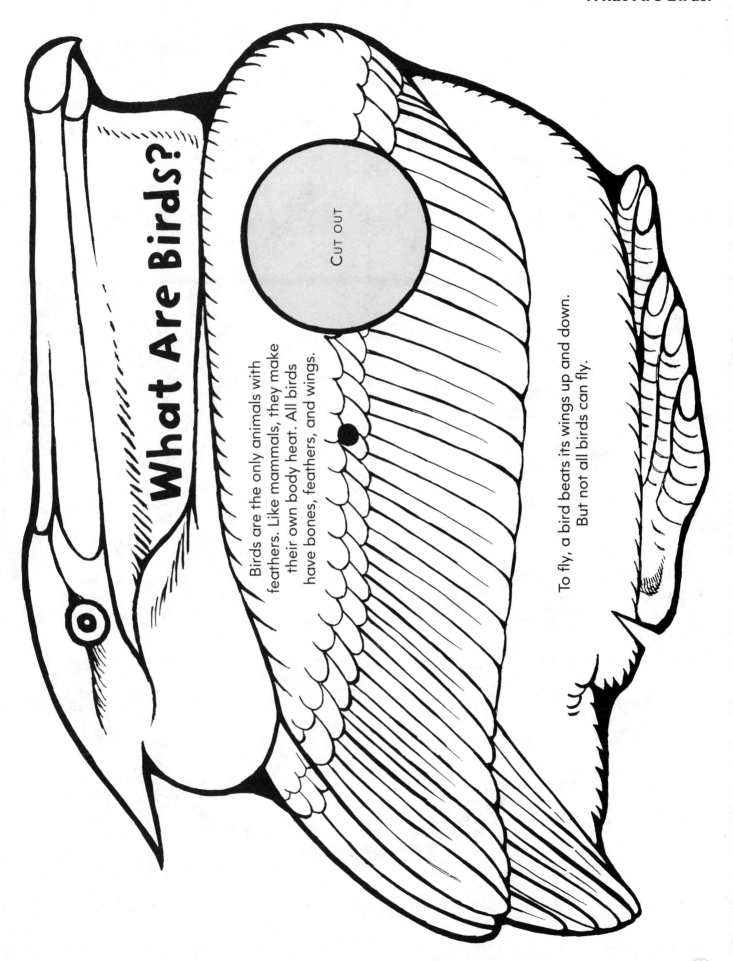

What Are Birds?

Birds are the only animals with feathers. Like mammals, they make their own body heat. All birds have bones, feathers, and wings.

Cut out

To fly, a bird beats its wings up and down. But not all birds can fly.

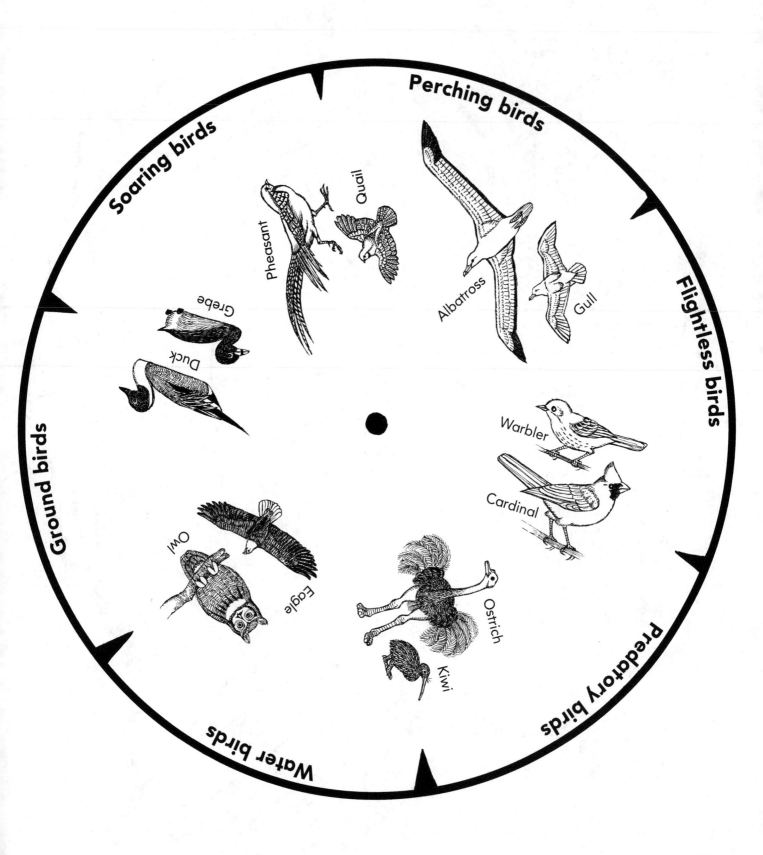

Perching birds

Soaring birds

Flightless birds

Ground birds

Predatory birds

Water birds

Pheasant

Quail

Grebe

Duck

Albatross

Gull

Warbler

Cardinal

Owl

Eagle

Ostrich

Kiwi

Interactive Science Wheels © 2013 by Donald M. Silver and Patricia J. Wynne, Scholastic Teaching Resources

What Are Reptiles?

This turtle-shaped wheel introduces snakes, lizards, crocodiles, and other cold-blooded reptiles.

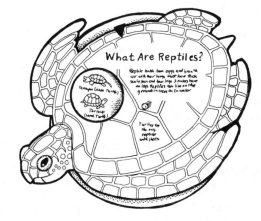

Science Corner

Reptiles are vertebrates (animals with backbones) that hatch from eggs and breathe air through lungs. Most reptiles have thick, scaly skin, which keeps water from escaping their bodies. This helps many reptiles thrive in hot deserts. Reptiles are cold-blooded—they cannot make their own body heat—so they depend on the sun to warm their bodies. There are more than 6,200 kinds of reptiles, all grouped into turtles, crocodiles, snakes, lizards, and tuataras.

Turtles are the only reptiles with shells. Most turtle shells are made of bony plates covered by a layer of scales. Some turtles have only a tough, leathery skin, but no shell. Instead of teeth, turtles use sharp-edged jaws to tear at the plants and animals they eat. Some turtles live in water, while others (known as tortoises) live on land. Some turtles can live more than 140 years and can weigh more than 500 pounds (225 kg).

Crocodiles and alligators are big, muscular reptiles with large heads, long tails, and powerful jaws. Crocodiles' teeth stick out of their closed mouths; alligators' teeth do not.

Snakes have no legs, but powerful muscles and special scales underneath their bodies help them climb trees, slither across the ground, and swim. They hunt rabbits, frogs, birds, lizards, and other snakes. Poisonous snakes inject deadly venom when they bite into their prey.

Some lizards, like the worm lizard, resemble snakes. But most lizards have long tails and four legs. While a few lizards feed on plants, most eat insects or spiders. Gila monsters are poisonous lizards that live in the desert. Other remarkable lizards include chameleons, which can change color to match leaves and branches; basilisk lizards, which can run across a stream without sinking; and Komodo dragons, which can grow up to 10 feet (3m) long! The lizard-like tuatara is one of a kind and is found only in New Zealand.

Dinosaurs are reptiles that lived millions of years ago then became extinct. Everything we know about dinosaurs today comes from bones, teeth, footprints, and other fossilized remains left behind when these animals died.

Materials

- ❋ reproducible pages 17 and 18
- ❋ scissors
- ❋ paper fastener
- ❋ colored pencils, crayons, or markers (optional)

More To Do

Heat Control

Reptiles can't make their own body heat so they rely on the sun to warm up. On a cool morning, for instance, a lizard will bask in the sun until its muscles have warmed up. When it becomes too warm, a lizard will rest in a shady spot. Have students draw two lizards on a piece of paper and cut them out. Tape a thermometer on each lizard. Place one lizard out in the sun and the other in the shade. After half an hour, have students check and record the temperatures of both lizards. Ask: *What is the difference between the two temperatures? Do you think the overall weather (a warm summer day vs. a cool spring or fall day) will affect how much difference there is in the temperatures?*

Resources

Lizards by Nic Bishop (Scholastic, 2010)

Eye-popping photographs put lizards—from the dwarf gecko to the Komodo dragon—in the spotlight in this fact-filled book.

National Geographic Readers: Snakes by Melissa Stewart (National Geographic Children's Books, 2009)

Easy-to-read text and colorful photos explore the world of amazing snakes.

http://dnr.wi.gov/org/caer/ce/ eek/critter/reptile/index.htm

This website features reptiles from Wisconsin. Click on the links to learn more about them.

Making the Wheel

1 Photocopy pages 17 and 18. Color, if desired.

2 Cut out the turtle and the wheel along the thick outer lines.

3 Cut open the CUT OUT window and the small triangular notch on the turtle along the thick solid lines.

4 Place the turtle on top of the wheel. Push the paper fastener through the centers of both pieces to join them, as shown.

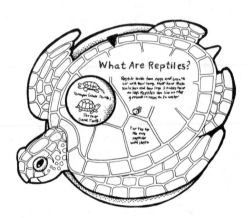

Teaching With the Wheel

Explain to students that snakes, lizards, turtles, and crocodiles are all reptiles. Invite them to share what they know about reptiles and make a list on the board. If any student mentions that dinosaurs were reptiles, include what students know about them on the list as well.

To learn more about reptiles, invite students to color, make, and read their wheels. Then check for understanding by asking them these questions:

1 What are reptiles? (*Reptiles hatch from eggs and breathe air with their lungs. Most have thick, scaly skin and four legs.*)

2 How are snakes and lizards alike and different? (*They are both reptiles and have scaly skin and tails. Lizards have four legs; snakes have none.*)

3 Which reptiles have shells? (*Turtles are the only reptiles with shells.*)

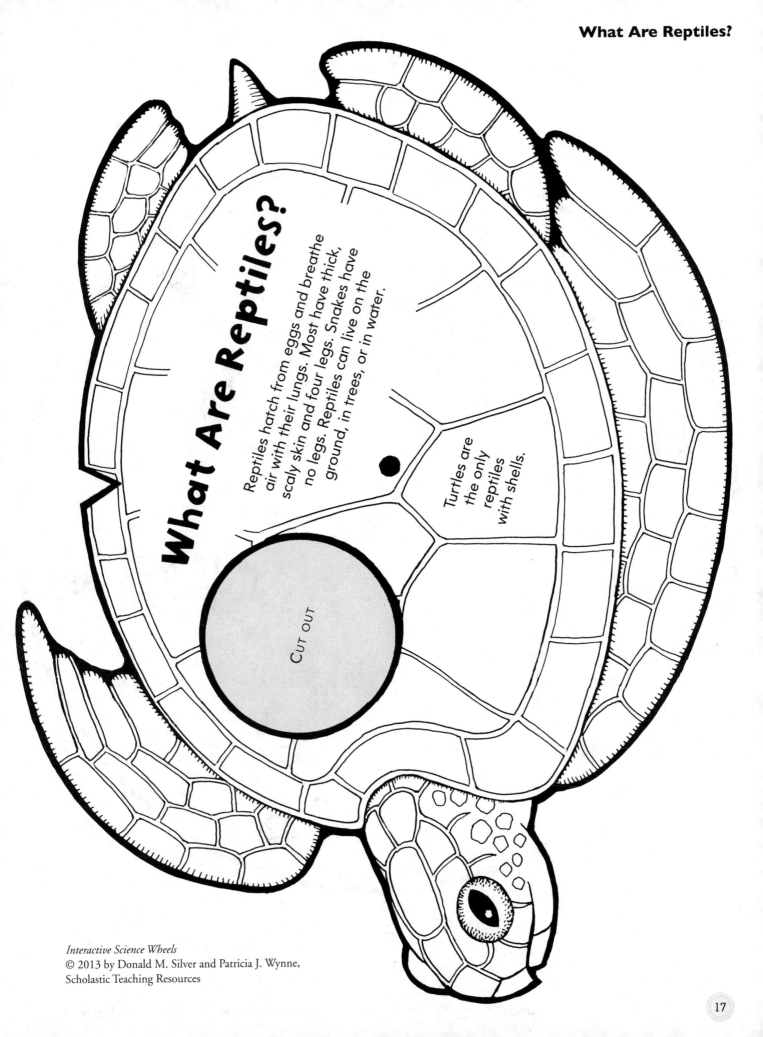

What Are Reptiles?

Reptiles hatch from eggs and breathe air with their lungs. Most have thick, scaly skin and four legs. Snakes have no legs. Reptiles can live on the ground, in trees, or in water.

Turtles are the only reptiles with shells.

CUT OUT

Interactive Science Wheels
© 2013 by Donald M. Silver and Patricia J. Wynne,
Scholastic Teaching Resources

Terrapin (water turtle)

Tortoise (land turtle)

Crocodile

Dinosaur

Snake

Lizard

Tuatara

Interactive Science Wheels © 2013 by Donald M. Silver and Patricia J. Wynne, Scholastic Teaching Resources

What Are Amphibians?

Get to know amphibians, such as frogs, toads, and salamanders, with this wheel.

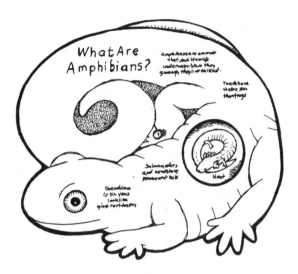

Science Corner

Amphibians are animals that live the first part of their lives in water, then change and grow into adults that can live and breathe on land. Because nearly all adult amphibians need to keep their thin, scaleless skin moist, they live close to lakes, ponds, or streams, or in damp woods or tropical rain forests. The three main groups of amphibians are frogs and toads, salamanders, and caecilians.

There are more than 2,600 kinds of frogs and toads. Toads are similar to frogs, but they usually have shorter legs. While frogs leap, toads make short hops. Toads have a thicker, drier skin so they don't have to live as close to water as frogs do. Toads and frogs start life as tadpoles, then undergo metamorphosis to become adults (see "A Frog's Life," page 35).

Salamanders include newts, olms, sirens, and mud puppies. There are more than 300 kinds of salamanders. When they hatch from their eggs, salamanders have tails that they keep for their entire lives. A few salamanders, such as olms, never lose their gills and spend their entire lives in water. Most salamanders, however, lose their gills and grow legs when they become adults. Many adult salamanders grow lungs but some have neither lungs nor gills. Instead they breathe through their thin, moist skins. Salamanders tend to live in damp places on land or in caves.

Caecilians have no legs and look like giant earthworms. Some swim in ponds and streams, while the rest live on land, burrowing in soil. Caecilians have tiny eyes that are covered with skin, giving the impression that they are blind. They can see, but their vision is probably limited to simply detecting dark and light. They use feelers to hunt for insects and other foods.

Materials

* reproducible pages 21 and 22
* scissors
* paper fastener
* colored pencils, crayons, or markers (optional)

More To Do

Break Point

Snakes often hunt salamanders to eat. But some salamanders have tails that break off when grabbed by predators, such as snakes. The snake gets the tail, but the salamander gets to escape. Later, the salamander grows a new tail. Invite students to research other ways amphibians protect themselves from predators. Have them focus on a specific amphibian, find out what its predators are, and what it does to escape from those predators.

Resources

Toad by the Road: A Year in the Life of These Amazing Amphibians **by Joanne Ryder (Henry Holt, 2007)**

Using watercolor and poetry, this beautiful book follows a toad's life through the four seasons.

Big Night for Salamanders **by Sarah Marwil Lamstein (Boyds Mills Press, 2010)**

Combining fiction and nonfiction, this picture book tells the story of how a young boy and his parents help spotted salamanders cross a dangerous road to get to their breeding ground.

http://dnr.wi.gov/org/caer/ ce/eek/critter/amphibian/ index.htm

Cool facts about frogs, toads, and salamanders can be found on this site, which includes a video of a scientist tagging salamanders.

Making the Wheel

1 Photocopy pages 21 and 22. Color, if desired.

2 Cut out the salamander and the wheel along the thick outer lines.

3 Cut open the CUT OUT window on the salamander along the thick solid line.

4 Place the salamander on top of the wheel. Push the paper fastener through the centers of both pieces to join them, as shown.

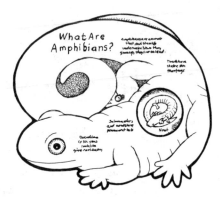

Teaching With the Wheel

Ask students if they have ever seen a frog, toad, or salamander. If so, where? What did it look like and what was it doing?

To learn more about amphibians, invite students to color, make, and read their wheels. Then check for understanding by asking them these questions:

1 What is an amphibian? (*An amphibian is an animal that starts its life underwater and then grows up to live on land.*)

2 Name five kinds of amphibians. (*Frog, toad, newt, salamander, caecilian*)

3 How are these animals alike and different? (*All are amphibians. Frogs and toads look alike, but toads have thicker skins. Newts and salamanders have permanent tails. Caecilians look like giant earthworms.*)

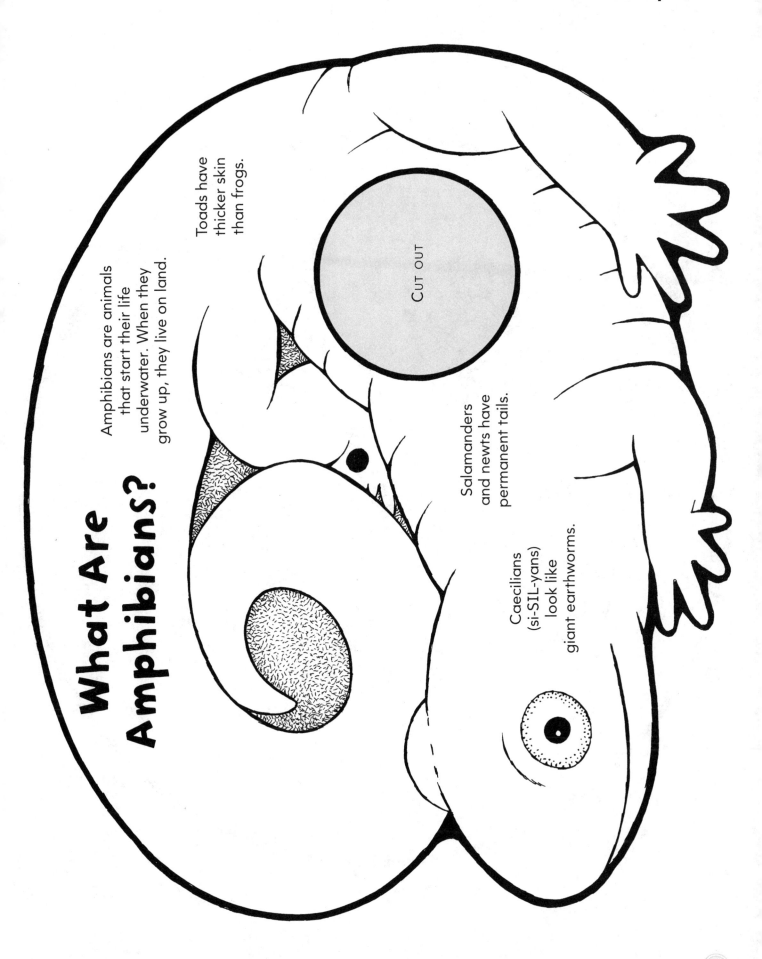

What Are Amphibians?

Amphibians are animals that start their life underwater. When they grow up, they live on land.

Toads have thicker skin than frogs.

CUT OUT

Salamanders and newts have permanent tails.

Caecilians (si-SIL-yans) look like giant earthworms.

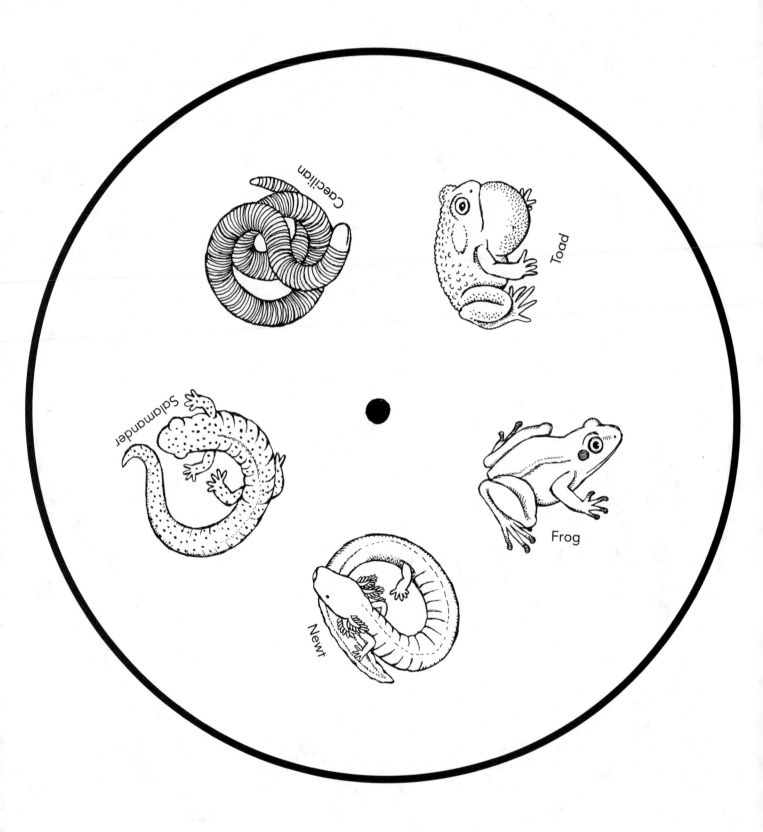

What Are Fishes?

Who knew fishes came in all shapes and sizes? Find out more with this wheel.

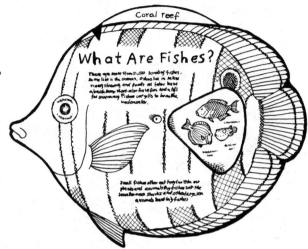

Science Corner

With more than 21,000 kinds, fishes make up the largest group of vertebrates—animals with backbones. The backbone is part of the skeleton, which is made up of strong, hard bone in most adult fishes. Adult sharks and rays, however, have skeleton made of cartilage, which is softer, lighter, and more flexible than bones.

Protecting most of a fish's body is a cover of tough, flexible scales that overlap one another, much like shingles on a roof. Only the head and fins are not covered by scales. The fins, along with the tail, help fish push through the water, steer itself, and keep balanced while swimming. Most fishes swim at a few miles per hour, but faster swimmers, such as tunas, can speed along for short bursts at more than 40 miles per hour. The more active a fish is, the more oxygen it needs. Fishes absorb oxygen from the water through their gills. Because fishes can't make their own heat, their body temperature is almost the same as that of the water around them.

Some fishes live in freshwater rivers and streams, while others thrive in the salty ocean—from surface waters to the deep-sea floor, in coral reefs or near the shore. Herrings and other small fishes as well as giant basking sharks feed on tiny floating sea plants and animals near the surface of the ocean. Large cods and mackerels prey on the small fishes and in turn become food for blue sharks and other predators. Many kinds of fishes lay millions of eggs at a time. Most of the eggs are eaten before they hatch and most of the baby fish that do hatch are eaten, too. Even so, enough survive to keep earth's waters teeming with billions of fishes.

Materials

* reproducible pages 25 and 26
* scissors
* paper fastener
* colored pencils, crayons, or markers (optional)

More To Do

Go Fish

Assign each student one of the fishes on the wheel. Challenge students to find out everything they can about their fish, draw a picture of it, and tell the class about it. Be sure they include how big each fish grows, where it lives, what it eats, and what eats it. Then, using this information, challenge students to make a food chain, starting with herrings that feed on tiny plants and animals, big fishes that eat herrings, and sharks that eat big fishes. Try to include as many of the fishes on the wheel as possible.

Resources

What's It Like to Be a Fish?
by Wendy Pfeffer (Collins, 1996)

This introductory book explains how a fish's body is adapted to life underwater.

Amazing Sharks by Sarah L.
Thomson (HarperCollins, 2006)

From learning about sharks, students also learn about how other fishes survive in the sea.

http://www.kidskonnect.com/
subject-index/13-animals/
30-fish.html

Start with the Fast Facts about fishes, then click on the many cool links to other sites.

Making the Wheel

1 Photocopy pages 25 and 26. Color, if desired.

2 Cut out the fish and the wheel along the thick outer lines.

3 Cut open the CUT OUT window and small triangular notch on the fish along the thick solid lines.

4 Place the fish on top of the wheel. Push the paper fastener through the centers of both pieces to join them, as shown.

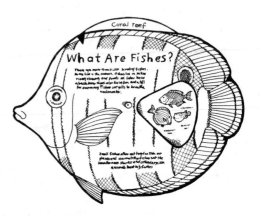

Teaching With the Wheel

Ask students if any of them have pet fishes or have seen fishes at an aquarium or at the beach. Have them describe the fishes they've seen—their size, color, and shape; what they were doing; what they eat; and so on.

To learn more about fishes, invite students to color, make, and read their wheels. Then check for understanding by asking them these questions:

1 What are some parts of a fish? (*Backbone, scales, fins and tail for swimming, gills for breathing*)

2 Where do fishes live? (*Some live in the oceans, others in lakes, rivers, streams, and ponds.*)

3 Name some freshwater fishes. (*Trout, sunfish, gar*)

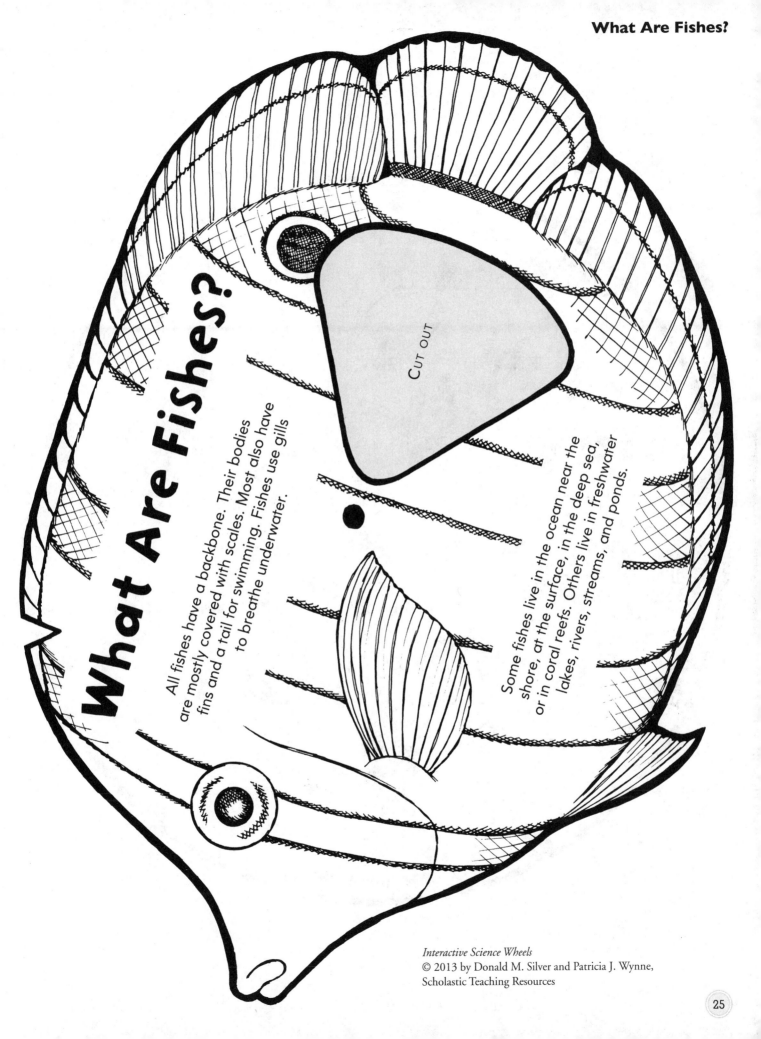

What Are Fishes?

All fishes have a backbone. Their bodies are mostly covered with scales. Most also have fins and a tail for swimming. Fishes use gills to breathe underwater.

Some fishes live in the ocean near the shore, at the surface, in the deep sea, or in coral reefs. Others live in freshwater lakes, rivers, streams, and ponds.

CUT OUT

Interactive Science Wheels
© 2013 by Donald M. Silver and Patricia J. Wynne,
Scholastic Teaching Resources

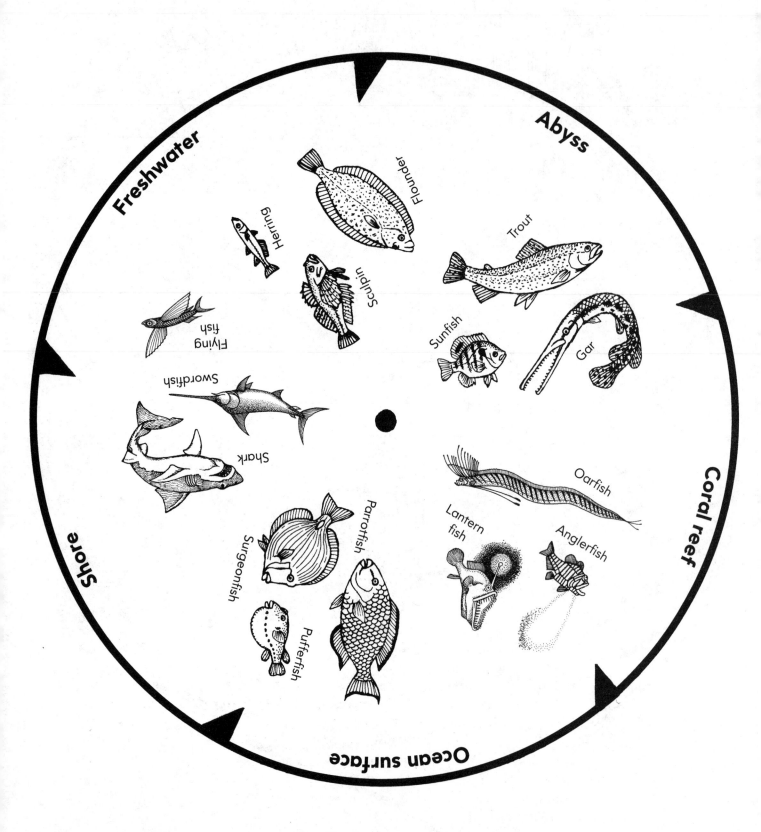

Interactive Science Wheels © 2013 by Donald M. Silver and Patricia J. Wynne, Scholastic Teaching Resources

What Are Invertebrates?

Discover a wide variety of invertebrates, or boneless animals—from one-celled amoeba to crustaceans.

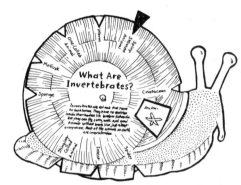

Science Corner

More than 97 percent of all the kinds of animals on earth have no bones in their bodies. They are called *invertebrates*, which means "animals without backbones." (Animals with backbones, called *vertebrates*, include fishes, amphibians, reptiles, birds, and mammals.) The smallest invertebrates are made up of just one cell. The largest are giant squids that can grow 12 feet (3.6 m) long with tentacles stretching 60 feet (18m). Invertebrates live just about everywhere—in oceans, on land, in rivers and lakes, inside caves, underground, and in the air. Some worms live inside other animals as parasites. There are more than 100,000 kinds of worms, including the familiar earthworm, which tunnels through soil, loosening and mixing it.

The vast majority of invertebrates are arthropods. Although arthropods have no bones, they have a hard covering on the outside that protects their segmented bodies. This outer covering has joints that allow tube-like legs to bend and move. Insects are arthropods with six legs; arachnids, such as spiders, have eight legs; and crustaceans, which include crabs, have ten legs. With more than one million species, insects are the largest group of arthropods and invertebrates. Ants, butterflies, bees, and beetles are all insects.

Just as insects have a hard outer cover, most mollusks have a shell that protects their soft bodies. Snails are mollusks with one coiled shell; scallops live inside a two-piece shell. A squid's shell is inside its body, while an octopus is a mollusk that lacks a shell.

Other sea-dwelling invertebrates include sponges—simple animals with porous bodies that allow water to flow in and out easily. Jellyfishes and sea anemones are invertebrates that use stings to attack prey. Echinoderms are spiny-skinned animals that include sea stars, sand dollars, and sea urchins.

Materials

- reproducible pages 29 and 30
- scissors
- paper fastener
- colored pencils, crayons, or markers (optional)

More To Do

Dig It

Take the class into the schoolyard or for a walk in the park. Bring along a tablespoon or some other digging tool and a piece of newspaper. Dig up some soil and place it on the newspaper, then have students watch for ants, worms, and other invertebrates moving around in the soil. Ask students to draw pictures of the creatures, but warn them not to touch the animals. Replace all the creatures and the soil. Back in the classroom, use a field guide or the Internet to try to identify the creatures.

Resources

Animals Without Backbones by Bobbie Kalman (Crabtree, 2007)

Simple text and photographs introduce kids to interesting invertebrates.

What Is an Arthropod? By Kathryn Smithyman and Bobbie Kalman (Crabtree, 2002)

Up-close photographs and labeled diagrams enable students to enter into the colorful world of invertebrates.

http://www.kidport.com/RefLib/science/Animals/AnimalIndexInv.htm

Learn about different kinds of invertebrates through this kid-friendly website.

Making the Wheel

1 Photocopy pages 29 and 30. Color, if desired.

2 Cut out the snail and the wheel along the thick outer lines.

3 Cut open the CUT OUT window and the small triangular notches on the snail along the thick solid lines.

4 Place the snail on top of the wheel. Push the paper fastener through the centers of both pieces to join them, as shown.

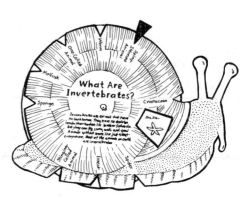

Teaching With the Wheel

Ask students: *What do worms, spiders, butterflies, and jellyfish have in common?* (These animals all don't have any bones in their bodies.) Challenge students to name other animals with no bones. Have them describe what the animal looks like, where it lives, what it eats, and so on.

To learn more about invertebrates, invite students to color, make, and read their wheels. Then check for understanding by asking them these questions:

1 How are all the animals on the wheel alike? (*Not one has a bone in its body.*)

2 Name five kinds of boneless animals. (*Answers will vary: sponges, stinging-celled animals, mollusks, worms, insects, spiders, crustaceans, spiny-skinned animals*)

3 What type of invertebrate is a crab? (*Crustacean*)

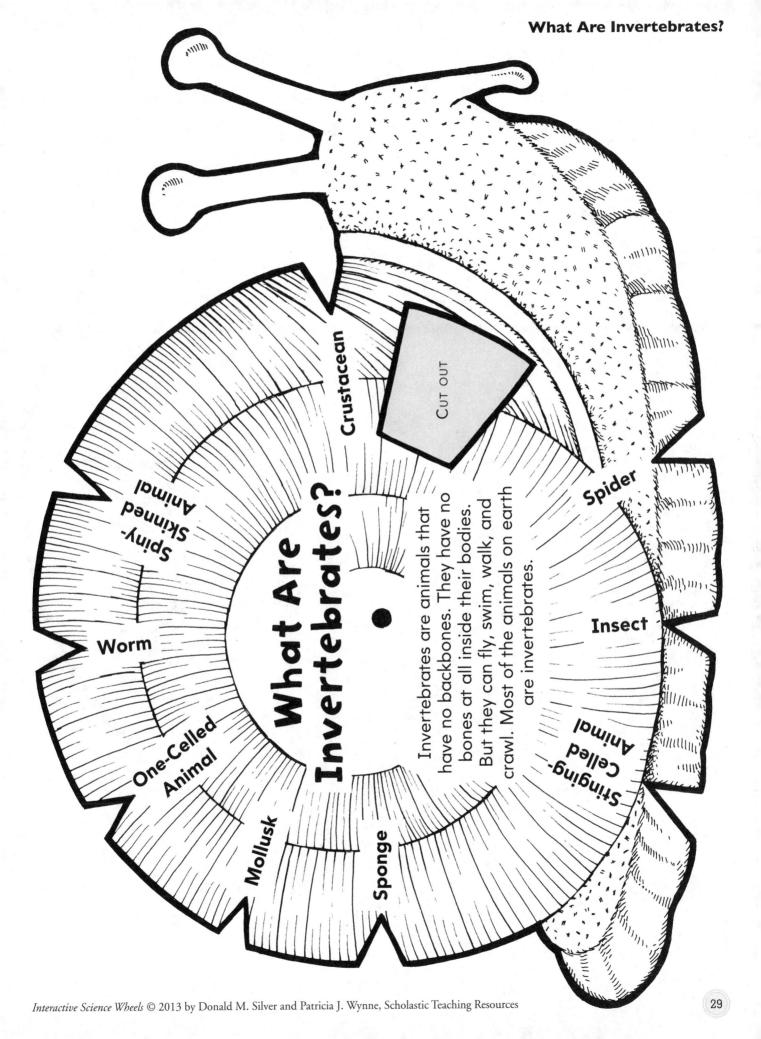

What Are Invertebrates?

Invertebrates are animals that have no backbones. They have no bones at all inside their bodies. But they can fly, swim, walk, and crawl. Most of the animals on earth are invertebrates.

CUT OUT

Crustacean

Spider

Insect

Stinging-Celled Animal

Sponge

Mollusk

One-Celled Animal

Worm

Spiny-Skinned Animal

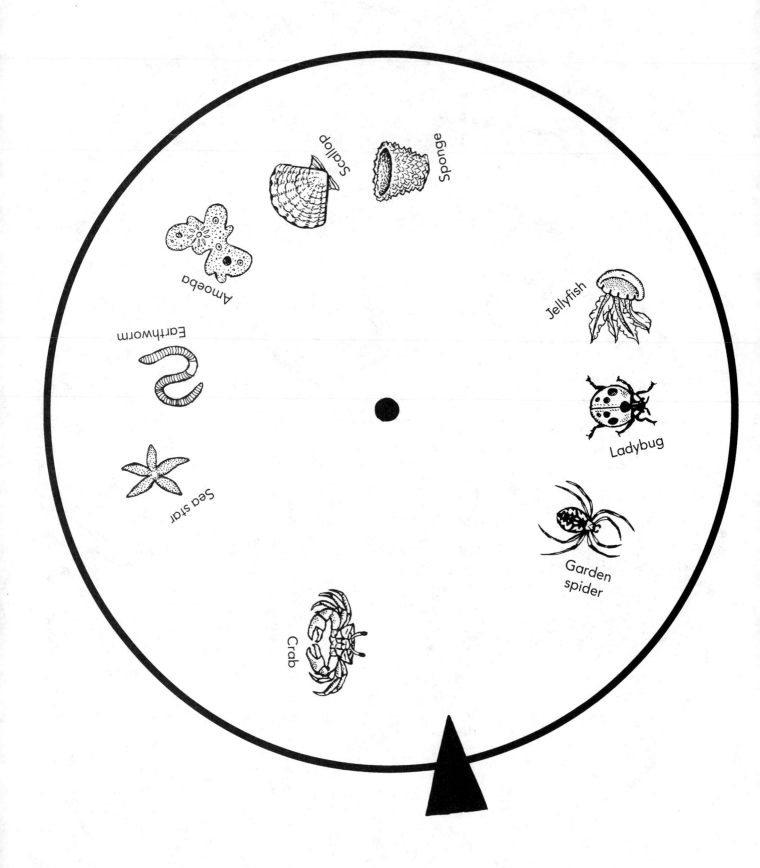

The Life of a Duck

Turn the wheel to see how a duck changes along with the seasons.

Science Corner

Ducks are water birds with broad, flat beaks, short tails, and waterproof feathers. Their webbed feet act like paddles for swimming in ponds, lakes, rivers, and streams. Even though they move gracefully in water, ducks waddle on land. Narrow, pointed wings help them fly quickly. Most ducks live together in flocks. In places that have cold winters, flocks of ducks fly off together in autumn and head to the warmer south. Then they return in the spring to mate, build nests, lay eggs, and raise their young.

A female duck can lay 6 to 15 eggs in the nest she builds. Each egg contains yolk, which provides all the food a baby duck needs to grow and develop. To keep her eggs warm, the duck pulls out soft, fluffy, down feathers from her breast and uses them to cover her eggs. After laying the last egg, the female sits on the eggs to incubate and protect them. Twenty-six days later, ducklings start to hatch. They come out of their eggs looking like their parents, only smaller and covered completely in down feathers. The mother duck leads her ducklings to water, where they immediately swim on their own. Some kinds of ducklings, however, climb onto their mother's back to be carried along as she swims. Throughout the spring and summer, ducklings eat and grow. Some ducks eat insects and snails, while others catch fish. Still others feed on seeds and grasses. Within five to eight weeks, ducklings learn to fly and are ready to join the flock when it migrates to its winter home. Ducks can live from 2 to 12 years, depending on the species.

Materials

* reproducible pages 33 and 34
* scissors
* paper fastener
* tape
* colored pencils, crayons, or markers (optional)

More To Do

Look Alikes

Many baby animals look like their parents when they are born or hatch out of eggs. Invite students who have pets to describe what their pet looked like when it was young. Ask: *Did it look a lot like its adult version?* Ask if anyone has a pet dog or cat that has had puppies or kittens. If so, invite students to bring in photos. What other baby animals can students think of that look like their parents? Have students bring in photos from magazines or printed from the Internet and make a chart. Ask students: *Did you look a lot or a little like your father or mother when you were born?*

Resources

Duck (See How They Grow) by Angela Royston (Dorling Kindersley, 2007)

Written from the duckling's point of view, this book uses close-up photos to show how a duckling grows.

A House for Wanda Wood Duck by Patricia Barnes-Svarney (Ducks Unlimited, 2002)

A family helps out a wood duck by building a nest box for it, then watches what happens next. Includes a simple diagram showing how to build a wood duck nest box.

http://www.kiddyhouse.com/Farm/ducks.html

This cute site provides answers to basic questions about ducks.

Making the Wheel

1 Photocopy pages 33 and 34. Color, if desired.

2 Cut out the ducks, the egg, and the wheel along the thick outer lines.

3 Cut open the CUT OUT window on the duck along the thick solid line.

4 Tape the duckling and the egg to the right of the text and webbed feet, as shown.

5 Place the duck on top of the wheel. Push the paper fastener through the centers of both pieces to join them, as shown.

Teaching With the Wheel

Ask students what they know about ducks. What do they look like? Where do they live? Where do baby ducks come from? What do ducklings look like? Invite students to draw pictures of ducks and write down everything they know about them.

To learn more about a duck's life cycle, invite students to color, make, and read their wheels. Have them turn the wheel clockwise. When the window reveals a picture, call on a student to read the text below. Then check for understanding by asking them these questions:

1 What is a duck? (*A duck is a water bird with waterproof feathers and webbed toes for swimming.*)

2 Describe a duckling. (*When ducklings hatch out of eggs, they look like their parents. They swim, eat, and grow.*)

3 Why do ducks fly in winter? (*They fly to warm winter homes.*)

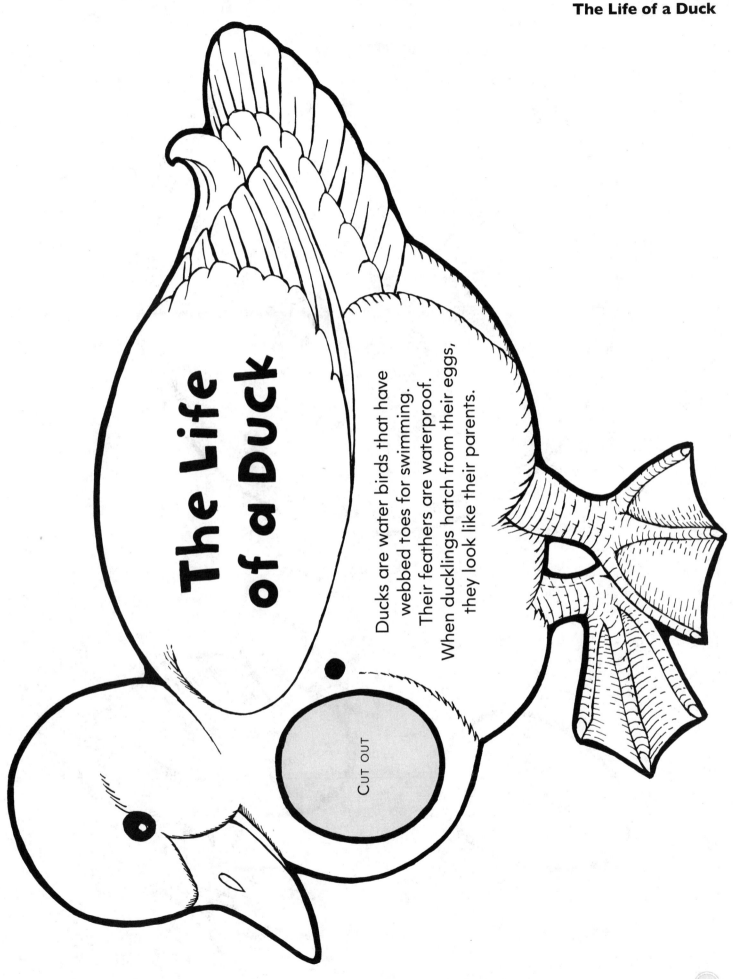

The Life of a Duck

Ducks are water birds that have webbed toes for swimming. Their feathers are waterproof. When ducklings hatch from their eggs, they look like their parents.

CUT OUT

The Life of a Duck

In spring, female ducks lay eggs in nests.

In the fall, ducks fly to warm winter homes.

Ducklings swim, eat, and grow.

Ducklings hatch from the eggs.

A Frog's Life

Follow the stages of a frog's life cycle to see how it changes as it undergoes metamorphosis.

Science Corner

Frogs are *amphibians*—they spend the first part of their lives underwater, but can live on land when they mature into adults. (See "What Are Amphibians?," page 19.) Many frogs lay their eggs in freshwater ponds. The eggs hatch into tadpoles that swim like fish and breathe through gills. They dine on small insects or water plants. After a few weeks, tadpoles start to turn into froglets, growing legs and developing lungs. Eventually their tail and gills disappear completely, and their metamorphosis into adulthood is complete.

Fully grown frogs breathe air through their lungs and use their powerful back legs for jumping or swimming. They hunt insects, spiders, worms, and snails, catching them with their long, sticky tongues. There are more than 2,600 kinds, or species, of frogs and toads. Toads are similar to frogs, but their legs are shorter and their skin is thicker and drier.

Materials

- reproducible pages 37 and 38
- scissors
- paper fastener
- tape
- colored pencils, crayons, or markers (optional)

More To Do

Frog Pond

Many frogs spend their lives in or near ponds. If you have a pond nearby, take the class for a visit and invite students to draw the plants and animals living there. Otherwise, bring in books that will introduce students to ponds and how pond life changes from season to season. Focus primarily on frogs and discuss their behavior, such as singing in the spring, sunning themselves on lily pads to warm up, hibernating through winter buried in the mud at the bottom of a pond, and so on.

Resources

***From Tadpole to Frog* by Kathleen Weidner Zoehfeld (Scholastic, 2011)**

Using vivid, full-color photographs, this book for beginning readers details a frog's life cycle.

***One Small Square: Pond* by Donald M. Silver and Patricia J. Wynne (McGraw-Hill, 1997)**

Readers take a look at a pond where frogs and other animals live, one small section at a time.

http://www.kiddyhouse.com/ Themes/frogs/

Full of fascinating facts about frogs, this site also contains links to other frog-related sites. Kids are sure to enjoy the frog games and activities.

Making the Wheel

1 Photocopy pages 37 and 38. Color, if desired.

2 Cut out the three main pieces along the thick outer lines.

3 Cut open the two CUT OUT windows on the frog along the thick solid lines.

4 Cut apart the four TAPE UNDER pieces.

5 Tape each piece under its matching letter on the wheel. Make sure the curve drawn on each piece lies directly under the curve of the wheel, as shown.

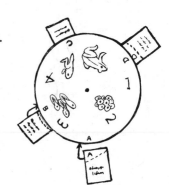

6 Place the frog on top of the wheel. Push a paper fastener through the centers of both pieces to join them, as shown.

Teaching With the Wheel

Ask students if they have ever seen tadpoles or frogs. Where? What did they look like? What were they doing?

To learn more about a frog's life cycle, invite students to color and make their wheels. Have students turn their wheels so the number "1" appears in the small window. Have them look at the picture and read the text on the tab at the bottom. Turn the wheel counterclockwise to 2, 3, and 4 and repeat. Then check for understanding by asking them these questions:

1 What hatches out of frog eggs? (*Frog eggs hatch into tadpoles that swim like fish.*)

2 How do tadpoles change? (*They grow legs and become froglets.*)

3 What happens to froglets as they grow? (*They lose their tails and become frogs.*)

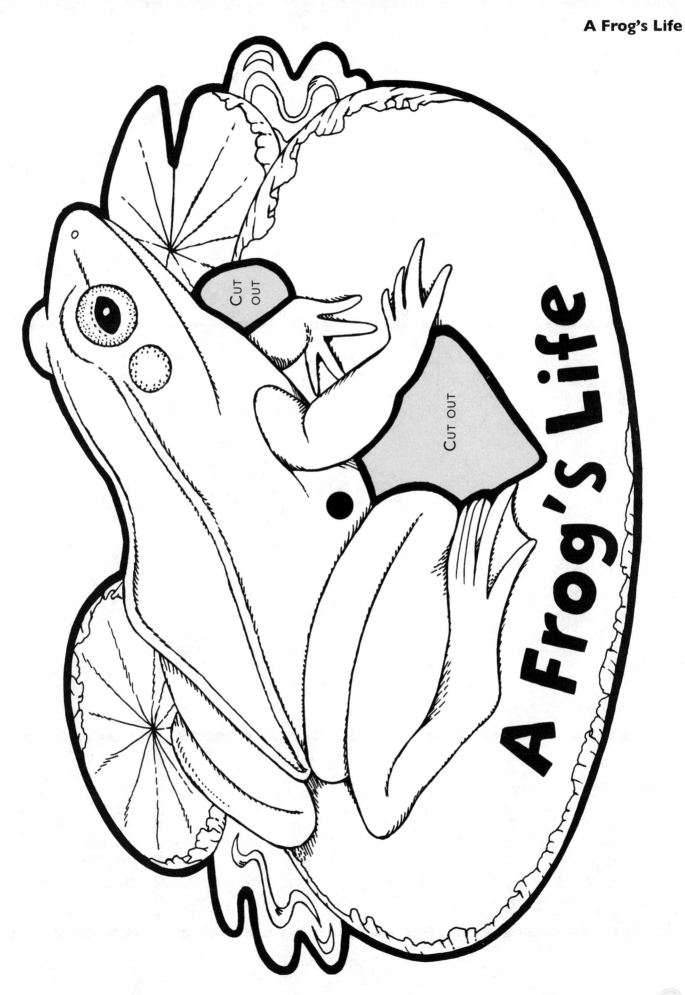

CUT OUT

CUT OUT

A Frog's Life

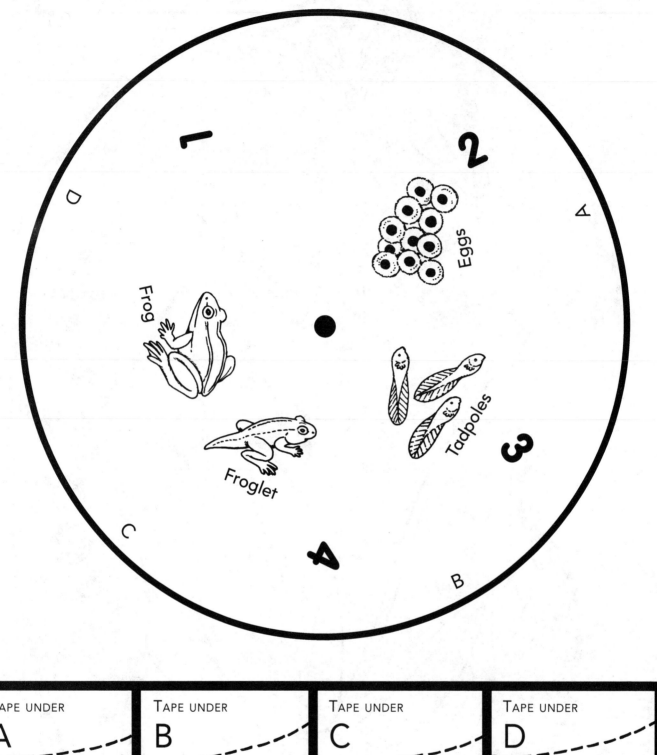

1

2

Frog

Eggs

Tadpoles

Froglet

3

4

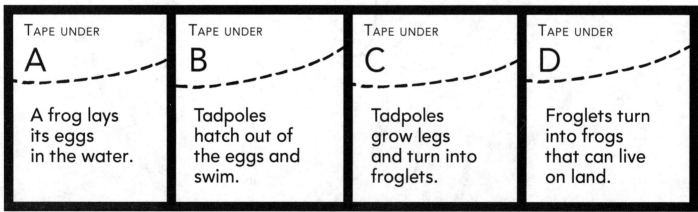

TAPE UNDER
A
A frog lays its eggs in the water.

TAPE UNDER
B
Tadpoles hatch out of the eggs and swim.

TAPE UNDER
C
Tadpoles grow legs and turn into froglets.

TAPE UNDER
D
Froglets turn into frogs that can live on land.

Interactive Science Wheels © 2013 by Donald M. Silver and Patricia J. Wynne, Scholastic Teaching Resources

Butterfly and Grasshopper Life Cycles

Lift the flaps to compare how a butterfly and a grasshopper change during their life cycles.

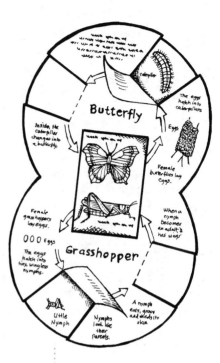

Science Corner

There are about a million kinds of insects, including butterflies, grasshoppers, bees, beetles, flies, and ants. All insects have six legs, no bones, and special mouthparts for eating different kinds of foods. Female insects lay eggs where they will be safe from other animals.

When a grasshopper hatches out of its egg, it looks like a smaller version of its parents, but without wings. Its mouthpart enables it to bite and chew leaves. As the young grasshopper (also called a *nymph*) continues to eat and grow, its body gets too big for its hard outer skin covering. When this happens, the nymph *molts*, or breaks out of its skin, and makes a new one. A nymph molts several times before it grows into a full-sized adult. During this molting stage, the young grasshopper develops wings. When it reaches full adult size, the grasshopper stops molting.

Unlike a grasshopper, a butterfly looks nothing at all like its parents when it hatches. A butterfly starts life as a multi-legged caterpillar (also known as a *larva*) and feeds on leaves. Like a grasshopper, a caterpillar molts as it grows. When a caterpillar has reached its full size, it stops eating and spins a silk "button" from glands near its mouth. It attaches the silk to a branch or other surface, and then hangs from it. The caterpillar then secretes a substance that hardens into a case called a *chrysalis* around its body. While inside the chrysalis, the caterpillar is called a *pupa*. It neither eats nor moves, but through the process of *metamorphosis*, its body transforms—growing wings, changing mouthparts, and developing six legs. When the change is complete, the chrysalis splits open and the full-grown butterfly pulls itself out. It pumps blood into its wings, waits for them to dry, then flies off to sip nectar from flowers, mate, and lay eggs.

Materials

* reproducible pages 41 and 42
* scissors
* tape
* colored pencils, crayons, or markers (optional)

More To Do

Big Change Artists

Butterflies aren't the only insects that change completely during their life cycles. Beetles, moths, and bees do, too. Challenge students to find out about these different kinds of insects and how they change from egg to adult. Make an insect chart on which students can write the names of different insects and draw pictures of them.

Resources

Are You A Grasshopper? by Judy Allen and Tudor Humphries (Kingfisher, 2004).

This easy-to-read book follows the life of a grasshopper living in a backyard.

From Caterpillar to Butterfly by Deborah Heiligman (Collins, 2008).

Students in a classroom watch as a caterpillar in a jar turns into a butterfly.

http://www. pacificsciencecenter.org/ exhibits/tropical-butterfly-house/faq

This site from the Pacific Science Center answers frequently asked questions about butterflies.

Making the Figure-Eights

1 Photocopy pages 41 and 42. Color, if desired.

2 Cut out the two figure-eights along the thick outer lines.

3 Cut open the CUT OUT window and the flaps on the BUTTERFLY & GRASSHOPPER piece along the thick solid lines.

4 Place the two figure-eights on top of each other so that the window reveals the pictures of the adult butterfly and grasshopper. Tape the figure-eights together at the top and bottom, as shown.

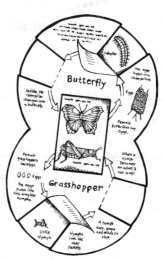

Teaching With the Wheels

Ask students if they have ever seen a butterfly or a grasshopper. Have them describe what the insects looked like, what they were doing, and where they were. Ask: *What do you think a butterfly looks like when it is young? What about a grasshopper?*

To learn more about a butterfly and grasshopper's life cycles, invite students to color and make their figure-eights. Have them follow the arrows, read the text, and lift the flaps. Then check for understanding by asking them these questions:

1 What kind of egg does a caterpillar hatch from? What about a nymph? (*A caterpillar hatches out of a butterfly egg; a nymph from a grasshopper egg.*)

2 How are caterpillars and nymphs alike? (*They eat, grow, and shed their skins.*)

3 What happens inside a caterpillar's hard case? (*The caterpillar turns into a butterfly.*)

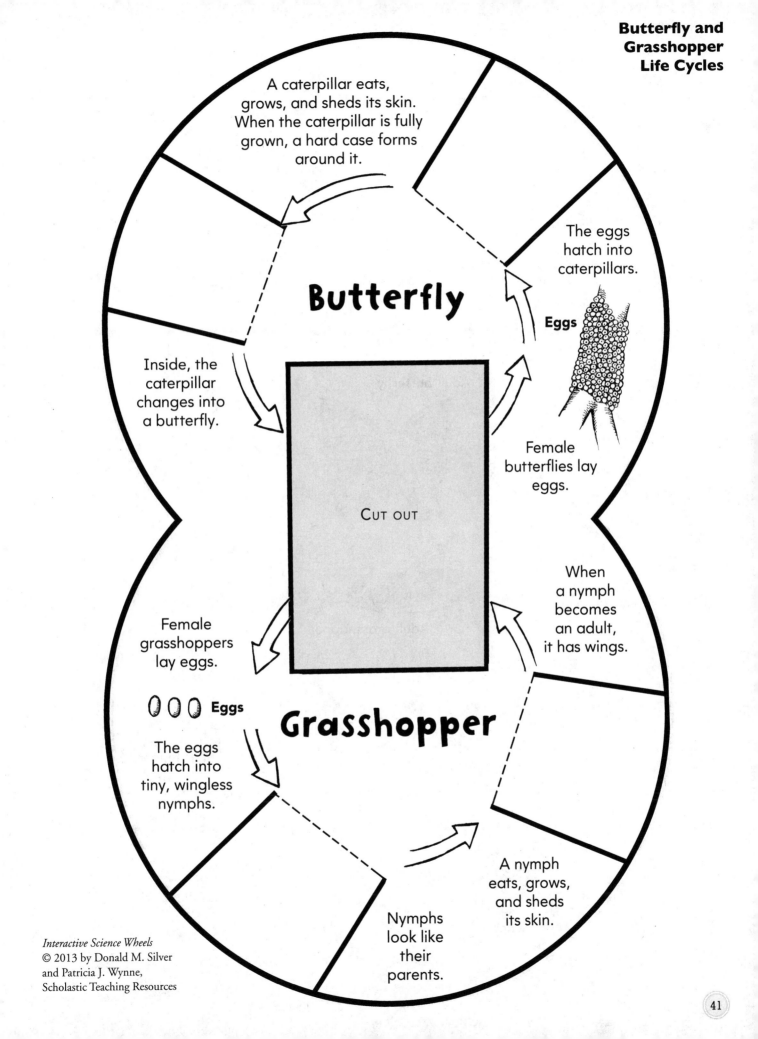

A caterpillar eats, grows, and sheds its skin. When the caterpillar is fully grown, a hard case forms around it.

The eggs hatch into caterpillars.

Butterfly

Eggs

Inside, the caterpillar changes into a butterfly.

CUT OUT

Female butterflies lay eggs.

Female grasshoppers lay eggs.

When a nymph becomes an adult, it has wings.

◖◖◖ **Eggs**

Grasshopper

The eggs hatch into tiny, wingless nymphs.

A nymph eats, grows, and sheds its skin.

Nymphs look like their parents.

Interactive Science Wheels
© 2013 by Donald M. Silver
and Patricia J. Wynne,
Scholastic Teaching Resources

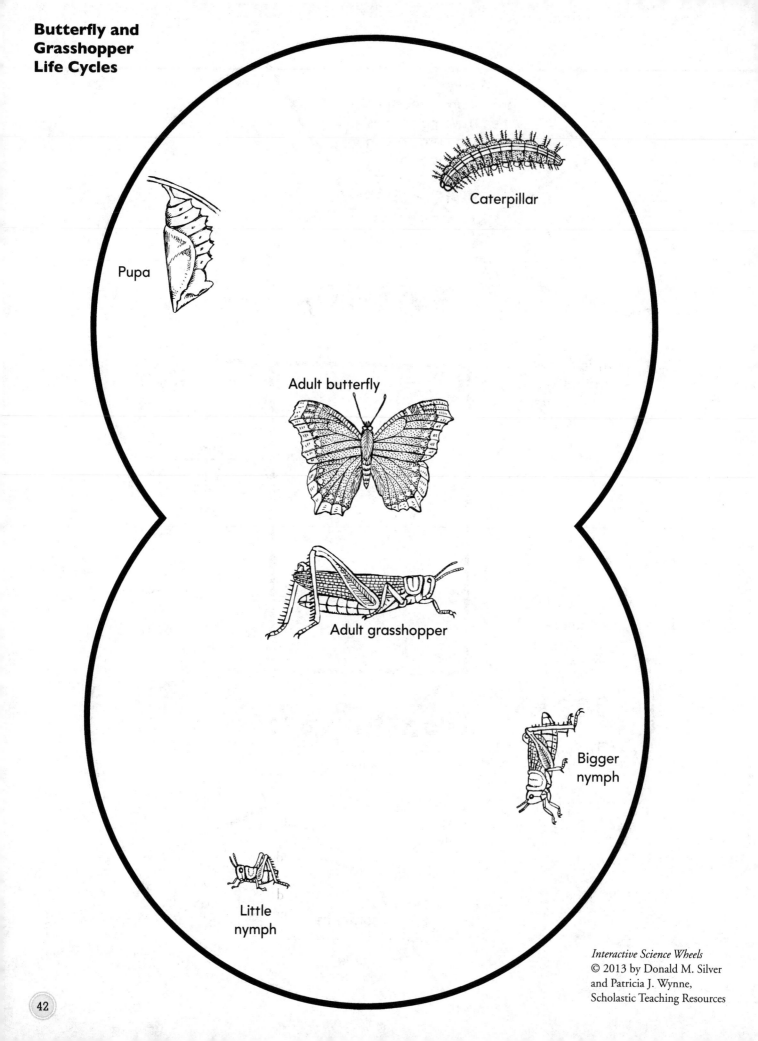

Butterfly and Grasshopper Life Cycles

Caterpillar

Pupa

Adult butterfly

Adult grasshopper

Bigger nymph

Little nymph

Interactive Science Wheels
© 2013 by Donald M. Silver
and Patricia J. Wynne,
Scholastic Teaching Resources

Parts of a Plant

**Turn the wheel to discover
the different parts
of a flowering plant.**

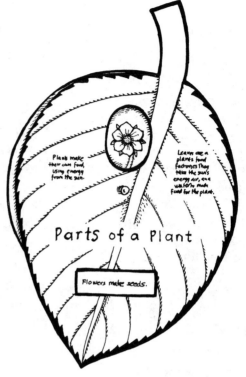

Science Corner

More than 350,000 kinds of plants grow on Earth. Nearly all of them have roots, stems, and leaves. Roots anchor plants to the ground and absorb water and minerals from the soil. Stems—which can be soft and pliable or hard and woody—carry the water and minerals from the roots to the leaves, support plants, and hold up leaves so they can absorb sunlight. Leaves contain chlorophyll, the chemical that captures the sun's energy and uses it to make food through the process of photosynthesis. When plants make food, they combine energy from the sun with water and carbon dioxide that they take in from the air. In the process of making food, leaves also make oxygen gas that they release into the air. Animals need oxygen to stay alive.

Most of the plants we see in gardens, parks, forests, and fields grow from seeds. In flowering plants, the flowers develop into fruits with seeds inside them. Cone-bearing plants, such as pines and cedars, have seeds inside their cones. Some plants, such as ferns, club mosses, and horsetails, do not make seeds. Instead, they release spores that grow into new plants.

Materials

* reproducible pages 45 and 46
* scissors
* paper fastener
* colored pencils, crayons, or markers (optional)

More To Do

Plant Part Pickup

Take the class for a walk and have students collect as many plant parts as they can find on the ground. Time the walk when deciduous trees, such as oaks and maples, are dropping their leaves. Students may also find pinecones, chestnuts, and seeds from flowering plants. When you return to the classroom, instruct students to tape each plant part to a sheet of paper. Have students label each part and write something about it. Display their findings on a bulletin board.

Resources

Plant Plumbing: A Book About Roots and Stems by Susan Blackaby (Picture Window Books, 2005)

Part of the Growing Things series, this basic book explains how roots and stems help keep plants alive.

I Wonder Why Pine Trees Have Needles by Jackie Gaff (Kingfisher, 2007)

Using a question-and-answer format, this book teaches about plants that grow in forests and the animals that interact with them.

http://www.backyardnature. net/botany.htm

Packed with facts and photographs, this site is a good source of information about all kinds of plants.

Making the Wheel

1 Photocopy pages 45 and 46. Color, if desired.

2 Cut out the leaf and the wheel along the thick outer lines.

3 Cut open the CUT OUT windows on the leaf along the thick solid lines.

4 Place the leaf on top of the wheel. Push the paper fastener through the centers of both pieces to join them, as shown.

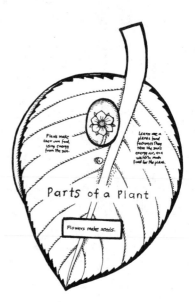

Teaching With the Wheel

Ask students to draw pictures of plants that they see in their homes or in the park. Have them label all the parts of the plants they can. (Answers will vary. Students should know that trees have trunks and leaves and that garden plants have stems, leaves, and flowers.)

To learn more about the parts of a plant, invite students to color, assemble, and read their wheels. Then check for understanding by asking them these questions:

1 Name at least three parts of plants. (*Seeds, leaves, fruits, flowers, stem, roots*)

2 What part of a plant makes food? (*Leaves make food using the sun's energy, air, and water.*)

3 What do roots do? (*They absorb water and minerals from the soil.*)

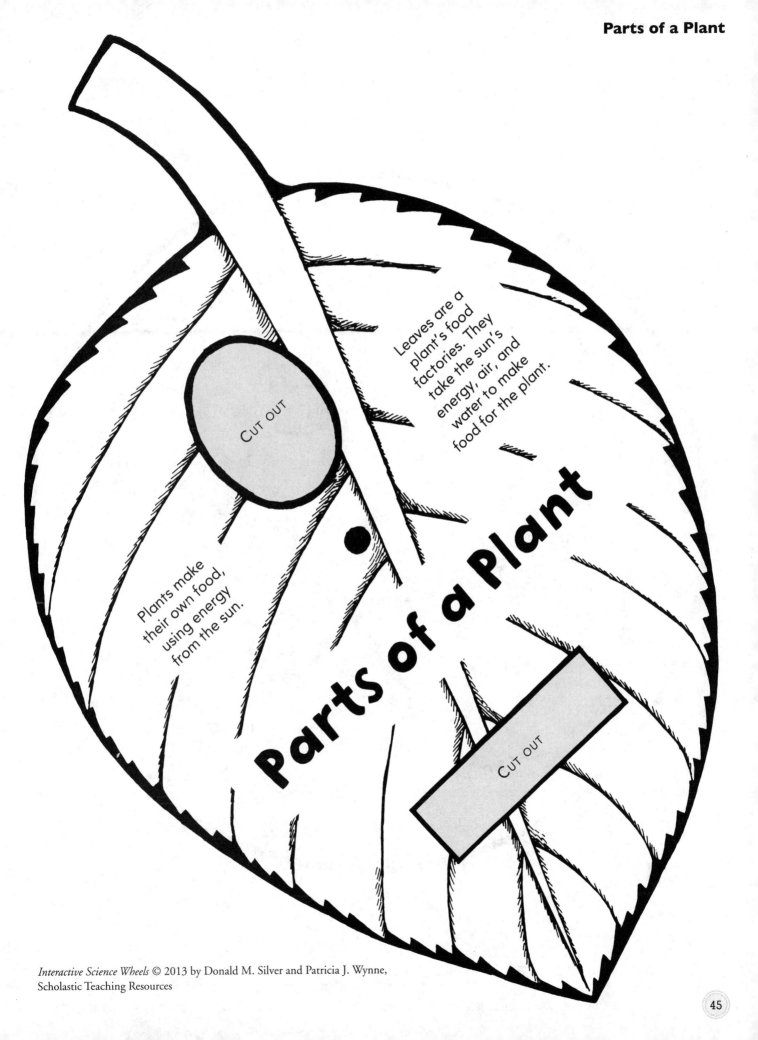

CUT OUT

Leaves are a plant's food factories. They take the sun's energy, air, and water to make food for the plant.

Plants make their own food, using energy from the sun.

Parts of a Plant

CUT OUT

Interactive Science Wheels © 2013 by Donald M. Silver and Patricia J. Wynne, Scholastic Teaching Resources

Parts of a Plant

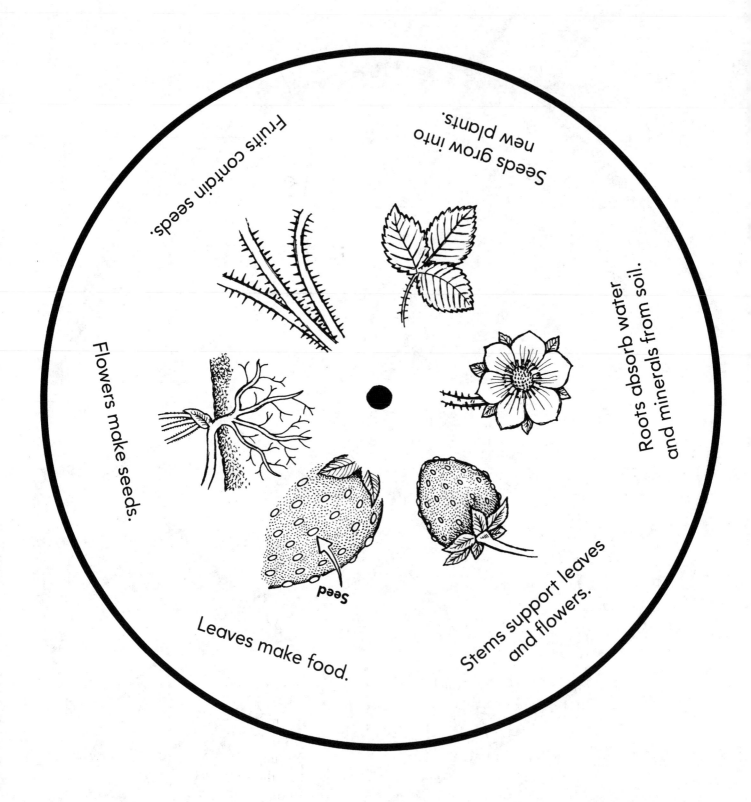

Fruits contain seeds.

Seeds grow into new plants.

Flowers make seeds.

Roots absorb water and minerals from soil.

Seed

Leaves make food.

Stems support leaves and flowers.

Interactive Science Wheels © 2013 by Donald M. Silver and Patricia J. Wynne, Scholastic Teaching Resources

A Sunflower's Life Cycle

From seed to flower, this wheel follows the growth of a sunflower.

Science Corner

Most plants grow from seeds. In flowering plants, the seeds develop inside flowers. (In pine trees and other evergreens, seeds form inside cones.) Male flower parts produce pollen, which must be carried to female flower parts by wind or animals in order to create seeds. A flower attracts bees, birds, and other pollinators with its bright colors, aromatic smell, and sweet nectar. As the animals fly from flower to flower, pollen sticks to their bodies and falls off on other flowers. When pollen reaches a plant's female parts, seeds are produced. The flowers then wither and fruits form containing the seeds.

Fruits help protect seeds and get them to good growing places. When an animal eats a juicy fruit, the seeds pass unharmed through the animal's digestive system and may be carried miles away before being dropped as part of the animal's waste. Some seeds have wing-like parts that catch the wind, while others have tiny hooks that stick to animals.

When a seed reaches a good growing spot and conditions are just right (e.g., enough water, warm temperatures, and so on), the seed germinates, or begins to grow, into a new plant. A young plant is called a seedling. The seedling's roots grow down into the ground to absorb water and minerals from the soil. Its stem grows up toward the light so its leaves can make food. Once the plant flowers, it can make seeds, and the whole process starts again.

Materials

* reproducible pages 49 and 50
* scissors
* paper fastener
* tape
* colored pencils, crayons, or markers (optional)

More To Do

Plant Watch

Invite students to select a plant that grows in their backyard, the schoolyard, or the park and watch it grow and change through the seasons. Have them draw pictures of the plant and keep a log of what happens to it. Does the plant flower? What animals, if any, visit the flowers? Does the plant lose its leaves in autumn? Encourage students to report their findings to the class.

Resources

The Tiny Seed by Eric Carle (Little Simon, 2009)

Vibrant illustrations and engaging text take readers on a journey following a seed as it is carried away by the wind to a growing place, where it develops into a new plant that flowers and makes more seeds. Comes with seeded paper so readers can grow their own flowers.

I Wonder Why Trees Have Leaves: And Other Questions About Plants by Andrew Charman (Kingfisher, 2003)

This charming question-and-answer book offers plenty of facts about the world of plants.

http://www2.bgfl.org/bgfl2/ custom/resources_ftp/client_ ftp/ks2/science/plants_pt2/ dispersal.htm

Click on the different dispersal methods to watch mini animations of how seeds travel away from their parent plants.

Making the Wheel

1 Photocopy pages 49 and 50. Color, if desired.

2 Cut out the four pieces, including the bird and bee pieces, along the thick outer lines.

3 Cut open the CUT OUT window on the sunflower along the thick solid lines.

4 Place the sunflower on top of the wheel. Push the paper fastener through the centers of both pieces to join them, as shown.

5 Tape the bird to the left side of the sunflower and the bee to the right.

Teaching With the Wheel

To learn about a flowering plant's life cycle, invite students to color, assemble, and read their wheels. Have them turn the wheel until the number 1 appears in the triangle. Have them keep turning the wheel in sequence to number 6. Check for understanding by asking them these questions:

1 What is a young plant called? (*Seedling*)

2 What makes seeds? (*Flowers*)

3 What spreads seeds? (*Birds*) What spreads pollen? (*Bees*)

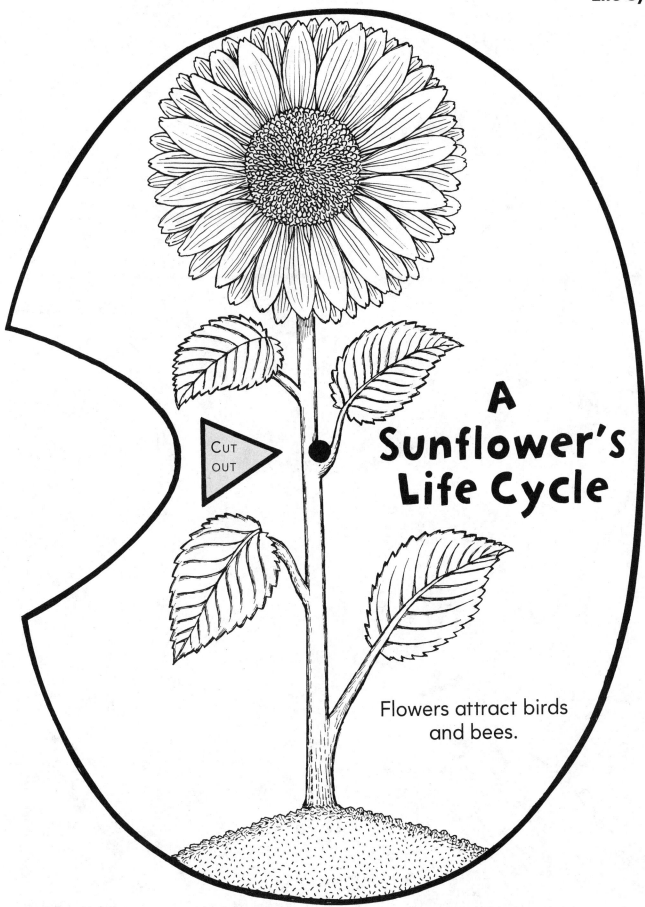

CUT
OUT

A
Sunflower's
Life Cycle

Flowers attract birds
and bees.

A Sunflower's Life Cycle

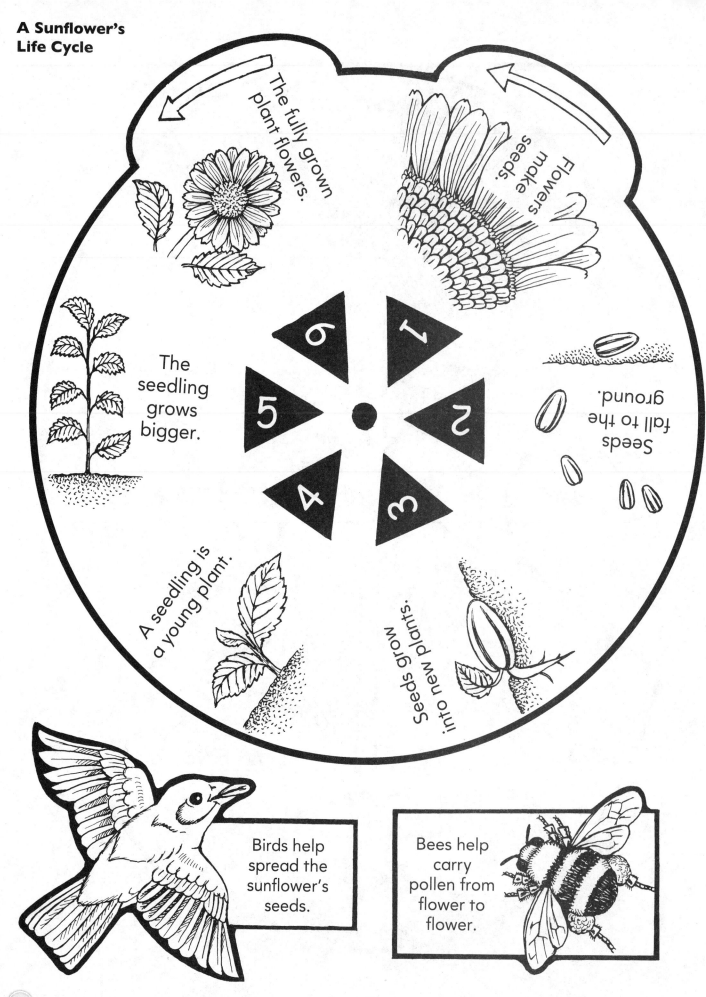

The fully grown plant flowers.

Flowers make seeds.

The seedling grows bigger.

Seeds fall to the ground.

A seedling is a young plant.

Seeds grow into new plants.

1
2
3
4
5
6

Birds help spread the sunflower's seeds.

Bees help carry pollen from flower to flower.

What Rock Is It?

Explore different kinds of rocks and learn how they formed.

Science Corner

Rocks are made up of one or more minerals, such as quartz, feldspar, calcite, and gypsum. Depending on how they formed, rocks are classified into three families: volcanic, or *igneous* rocks; layered, or *sedimentary* rocks; and changed, or *metamorphic* rocks.

Volcanic rock forms from hot lava that flows out of volcanoes. When the lava cools, it hardens into solid rock, called igneous, from the Latin word *ignis* for "fire." Granite is the most common igneous rock found on land, while basalt is often found on the seafloor. The minerals in granite—quartz, mica, feldspar, and hornblende—make it hard enough to be used in buildings.

Over time, as a result of weathering, igneous rocks can break and crumble into bits and pieces called sediment. Rain washes sediment into rivers, which carry it to the sea. The sediment settles to the bottom of the ocean floor and piles up, layer upon layer, with the upper layers pressing down on the lower ones. After millions of years, the lower layers become pressed and cemented into layered or sedimentary rocks, such as limestone, sandstone, and coal.

In places where there is great heat and pressure, such as where mountains rise or earthquakes occur, changed or metamorphic rocks form. Under such high heat and pressure, limestone changes into marble, granite changes into gneiss (pronounced "nice"), and basalt into mica schist.

When metamorphic and sedimentary rocks undergo weathering, they also break and crumble into sediment that forms new layered rocks. Deep inside the earth, igneous, sedimentary, and metamorphic rocks can melt to form a mixture of minerals and gases that flows out of volcanoes as lava and hardens into new volcanic rocks. The way in which one kind of rock changes into another is known as the *rock cycle*.

Materials

- reproducible pages 53 and 54
- scissors
- 3 paper fasteners
- colored pencils, crayons, or markers (optional)

More To Do

Rock Charts

Divide the class into three groups. Assign the first group the following rocks: tuff, pumice, and gabbro. Assign the second group chalk, shale, and conglomerate. Assign the third slate, quartzite, and anthracite. Challenge each group to find out if their rocks are igneous, sedimentary, or metamorphic. Have each group make a chart showing the name of their rocks, what the rocks look like, and what kind of rocks they are.

Resources

***Looking At Rocks* by Jennifer Dussling (Grosset and Dunlap, 2001)**

This easy-to-read book is an excellent introduction to different kinds of rocks and how they are formed.

***The Best Book of Fossils, Rocks, and Minerals* by Chris Perrault (Kingfisher, 2000)**

Realistic illustrations and simple text help young readers understand what rocks and minerals are and how fossils formed in sedimentary rocks.

http://www.rocksforkids.com

Click on "Pictures of Rocks" to find photos of many rocks and minerals, as well as fascinating facts about each one.

Making the Wheel

1 Photocopy pages 53 and 54. Color, if desired.

2 Cut out the four pieces along the thick outer lines.

3 On the largest piece, cut open the six CUT OUT windows and three small triangular notches along the thick solid lines.

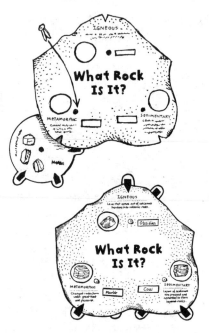

4 Place the small IGNEOUS ROCKS wheel under the IGNEOUS section of the big piece, as shown. Push a paper fastener through the black dots on both pieces and secure.

5 Repeat Step 4 with the SEDIMENTARY ROCKS wheel and the METAMORPHIC ROCKS wheel.

Teaching With the Wheel

Explain to students that rocks can change from one kind of rock to another kind (for example, limestone, which is a sedimentary rock, changes into marble, which is a metamorphic rock). The ways in which this happens make up the rock cycle.

To learn more about rocks, invite students to color, make, and read their wheels. Have students turn the wheels and name each of the rocks. Point out the gneiss is pronounced "nice." Then check for understanding by asking them these questions:

1 What are the main kinds of rocks? (*Igneous, sedimentary, and metamorphic*)

2 What kind of rocks form under great heat and pressure? (*Metamorphic rocks*)

3 What are some examples of sedimentary rocks? (*Answers will vary, but could include limestone, coal, and sandstone*)

What Rock Is It?

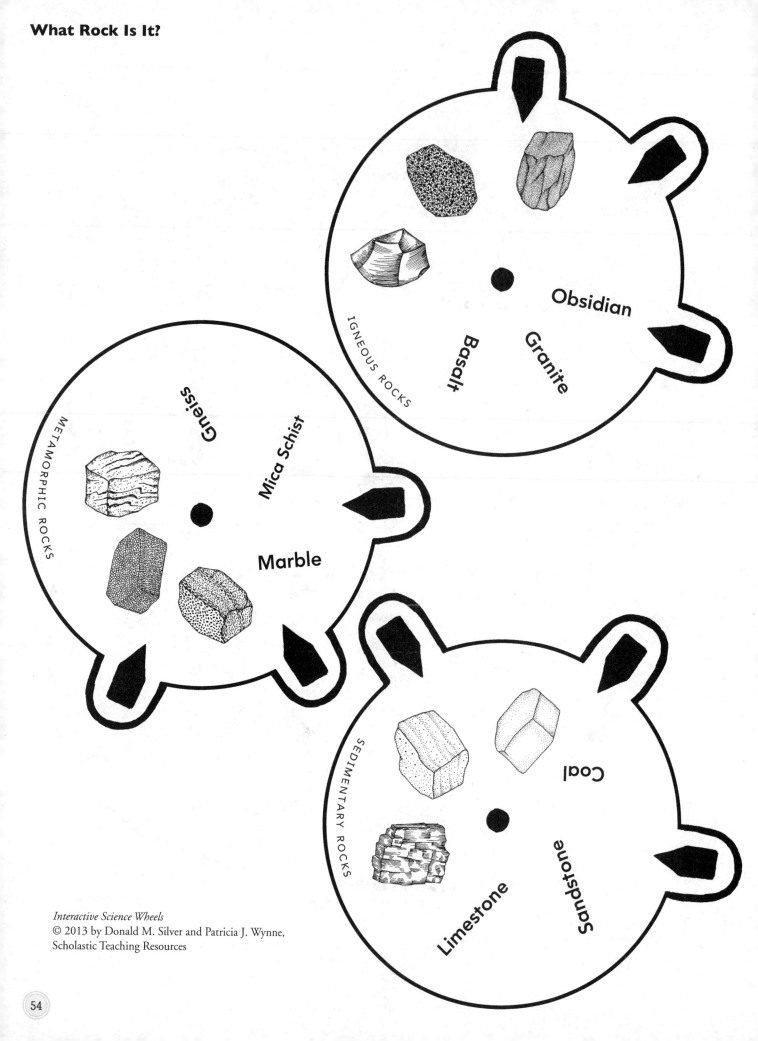

IGNEOUS ROCKS

Obsidian

Granite

Basalt

METAMORPHIC ROCKS

Gneiss

Mica Schist

Marble

SEDIMENTARY ROCKS

Coal

Limestone

Sandstone

The Changing Moon

Observe how the moon seems to change shape throughout the month.

Science Corner

The moon is Earth's closest neighbor in space. It circles our planet once about every 28 days. Unlike the sun, the moon cannot make its own light. The light we see from the moon is actually sunlight reflecting off its surface and bouncing toward Earth. The sun lights only half of the moon at a time. Depending on where the moon is in its orbit around our planet, different parts of the moon can be seen from Earth.

From our vantage point, the light reflecting off the moon gives the moon different shapes, or *phases*. When the moon is between the sun and Earth, its dark side faces Earth. During this phase, which we call "new moon," we cannot see the moon because there is no sunlight reflecting off the side facing Earth. As the moon continues to circle around the Earth, we begin to see more and more of the moon's sunlit side. First, we see a sliver (or *crescent*), which eventually grows (or *waxes*) into a half moon (called a *quarter moon*, because it is one-quarter of the way around its orbit of the Earth), then a full moon. After the full moon, we see progressively less of the moon (*waning*) as it continues its orbit around our planet, until it starts the new-moon phase again.

Materials

* reproducible pages 57 and 58
* scissors
* paper fastener
* colored pencils, crayons, or markers (optional)

More To Do

Sizing Up the Moon

When the full moon is low in the sky, it looks very big. Later, when it has moved higher, the moon looks smaller. Does the moon change its size? Encourage students to find out. On the next full moon, give each student a large paper clip. Help them open the paper clip into a "V" shape. Instruct students to go outside soon after sunset with an adult and find the moon. It should be low on the horizon. Have them hold the paper clip at arm's length so that the moon is inside the V. Bend the sides of the V so the moon fits inside. About two hours later, when the moon is higher in the sky, have students go outside to look at the moon and measure it again with the V. Does it still fit inside? (*It will.*)

Resources

Phases of the Moon by Gillia M. Olson (Capstone, 2008)

This book's simple text and clear photographs identify the phases of the moon and explain why they occur.

Faces of the Moon by Bob Crelin (Charlesbridge, 2009)

Written in verse and filled with die-cut holes, this ingenious book helps students see understand why the moon changes shape.

http://www.woodlands-junior.kent.sch.uk/time/moon/phases.html

This site has it all—from the moon's phases to tips for moon watching to moon facts. Note that while the times and dates are for the United Kingdom, the clear explanations are universal.

Making the Wheel

1 Photocopy pages 57 and 58. Color, if desired.

2 Cut out the circles along the thick outer lines.

3 Cut out the window in the smaller circle along the thick solid lines.

4 Place the smaller circle on top of the bigger wheel. Push the paper fastener through the centers of both circles to join them, as shown.

Teaching With the Wheel

Invite students to draw what the moon looked like the last time they saw it. Have them hold up their drawings. If all students drew only one phase of the moon (for example, full moon), draw other phases (crescent or quarter moon) on the board and ask if anyone has ever seen the moon look like those shapes.

To learn more about the phases of the moon, invite students to color, make, and read their wheels. Explain that the wheel shows the moon's phases over 28 days. Then check for understanding by asking them these questions:

1 Does the moon actually change shape? (*No, it just looks like it.*)

2 Why does the moon look like it changes shape? (*We see only the part of the moon that is lit by the sun.*)

3 In which phase of the moon can we see a complete circle? (*Full*)

The Changing Moon

Do you watch the moon in the night sky?
Does it always look the same?
Turn the circle to see. The moon seems to
change shape. But it really doesn't. We see only
the part of the moon that is lit by the sun.

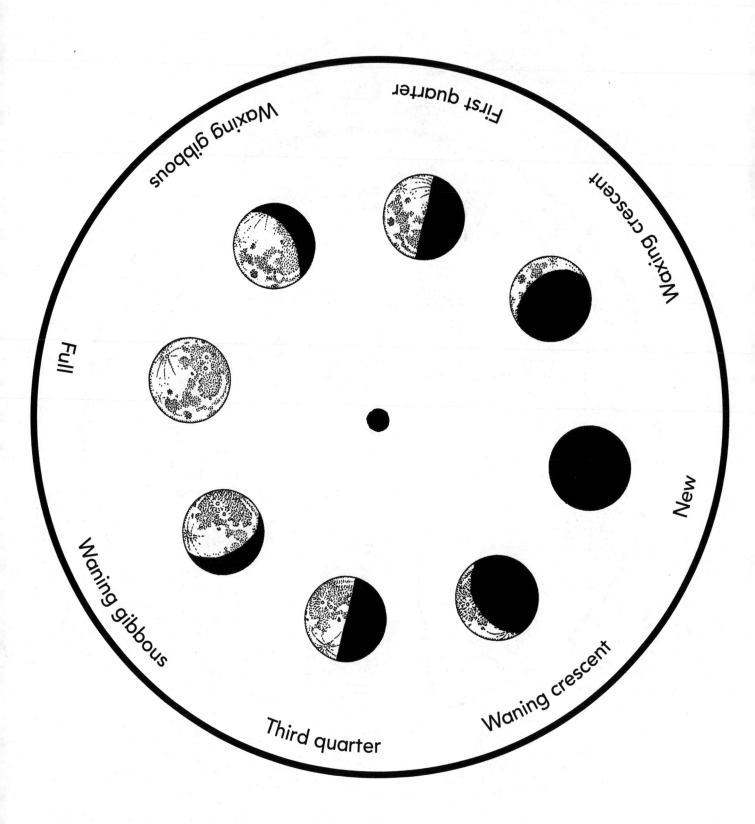

What's in the Night Sky?

There's more to the night sky than the moon and stars. Discover what else you can see with this wheel.

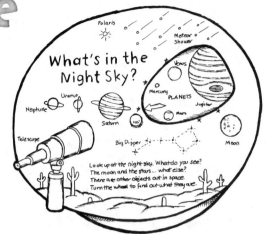

Science Corner

Students know that when they look at the night sky they can see stars and the moon. They may not know that sometimes they can also see planets, meteorites, and comets. On a clear dark night, away from city lights, it is possible to see about 2,000 stars. With the help of a telescope, many thousands more become visible.

Stars are immense fiery balls of gas that produce their own light. The sun is the closest star to Earth and the only star in our solar system. Our sun is a medium-sized yellow star that appears bigger and brighter than other stars because it is only 93 million miles (150 million km) away. Many stars in the night sky are bigger and brighter. Stars are often grouped into *constellations*, which ancient stargazers named for animals. The constellation Ursa Major, for example, looked like a great bear. Some of the stars in Ursa Major form the shape of a Big Dipper. The stars that make up a constellation appear to be close together, but they are actually millions of miles away from one another.

Unlike stars, planets and moons don't make their own light. They can be seen in the night sky because they reflect light from the sun back to Earth. Because the planets appear to wander across the night sky, they were named after the Greek word for "wanderer." Eight planets orbit the sun in the solar system: Mercury, Venus, Earth, Mars, Jupiter, Saturn, Uranus, and Neptune. (Pluto is considered a dwarf planet.) Moons orbit most of the planets in our solar system. Earth has one moon, Mars has two, and Saturn has at least twenty.

On some nights, we can see streaks of light shoot across the sky. People often call them "shooting stars," but they are actually *meteors*—chunks of rock or metal that drift through space and burn up when they enter Earth's atmosphere. *Comets*, which may also streak across the sky, are balls of ice, frozen gases, and rock that travel around the solar system. When one approaches close to the sun, the comet heats up and glows, forming a long tail of dust and gas. *Asteroids* are also chunks of rock and metal that orbit our sun, between Mars and Jupiter, and can be seen only with a telescope.

Materials

* reproducible pages 61 and 62
* scissors
* paper fastener
* colored pencils, crayons, or markers (optional)

More To Do

Star Search

Look in a newspaper or on the Internet for a star chart that shows which stars are visible from your town or city. Make copies of the chart for students. Ask students to go outdoors with an adult soon after sunset and try to find some of the constellations on the star chart. For example, Orion the Hunter is a constellation that can be seen in the northern hemisphere. The three stars in Orion's belt can be seen even in cities where light from buildings makes it difficult to see most other stars.

Resources

***Don't Know Much About the Solar System* by Kenneth C. Davis (HarperCollins, 2004)**

Using a question-and-answer format, this book introduces the solar system, as well as stars, constellations, and galaxies.

***Find the Constellations* by H.A. Rey (HMH Books, 2008)**

The author of the Curious George books shows his passion for astronomy with this kid-friendly guide to the constellations. Updated to include new scientific information, this book will help even the youngest students find constellations in the night sky. Sky charts are an added bonus.

http://www.kidscosmos.org/ cosmos/cosmos_star_maps.php

Find out which stars are visible in the night sky every month of the year. Links offer more information about stars, galaxies, and other objects in the night sky.

Making the Wheel

1 Photocopy pages 61 and 62. Color, if desired.

2 Cut out the oval piece and the wheel along the thick outer lines.

3 Cut open the CUT OUT window on the oval piece along the thick solid line.

4 Place the oval on top of the wheel. Push the paper fastener through the centers of both pieces to join them, as shown.

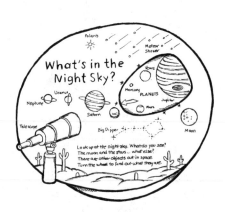

Teaching With the Wheel

Ask students what they saw the last time they looked up at the night sky. (*Answers will vary. Most students should have seen the moon and some stars; some may have seen the planet Venus but thought it was a star.*) Discuss how some objects in the night sky can be easily seen with their bare eyes or with a pair of binoculars; but to see other objects, they would need a telescope. Point to the telescope on the wheel and explain that this instrument helps us see objects that are much farther away.

To learn more about the night sky, invite students to color, assemble, and read their wheels. Then check for understanding by asking them these questions:

1 What are Mercury, Venus, Mars, and Jupiter? (*Planets*)

2 Name an example of a star. (*Answers will vary; possible answers include Rigel and Betelgeuse*)

3 Name a constellation. (*Answers will vary; possible answers include Canis Major and the Big Dipper*)

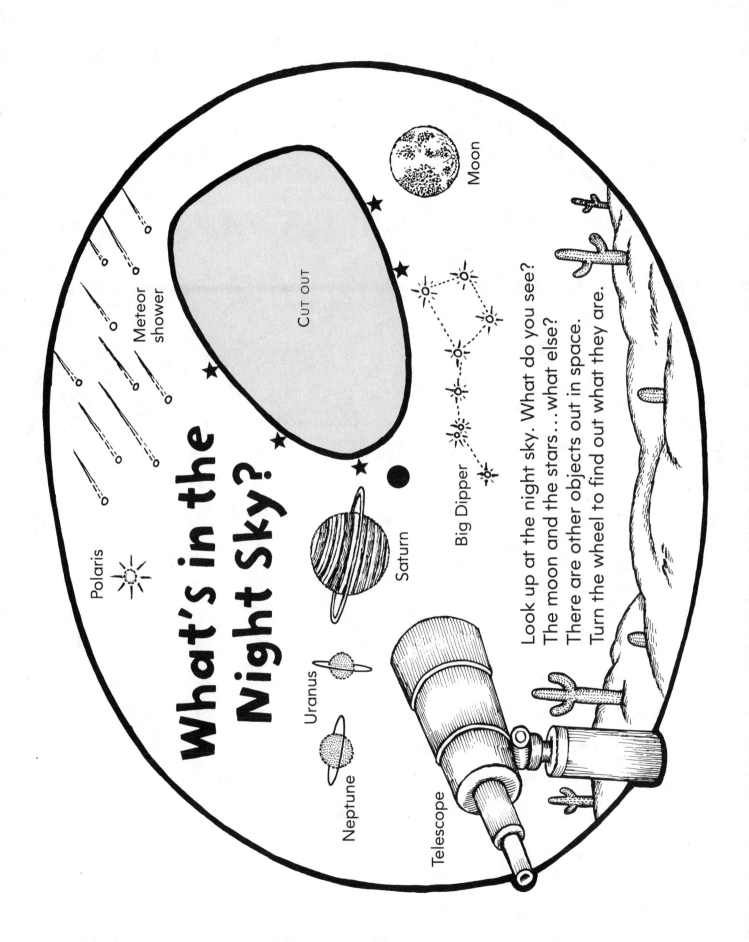

Meteor shower

CUT OUT

Moon

Polaris

What's in the Night Sky?

Saturn

Big Dipper

Uranus

Neptune

Telescope

Look up at the night sky. What do you see?
The moon and the stars…what else?
There are other objects out in space.
Turn the wheel to find out what they are.

What's In the Night Sky?

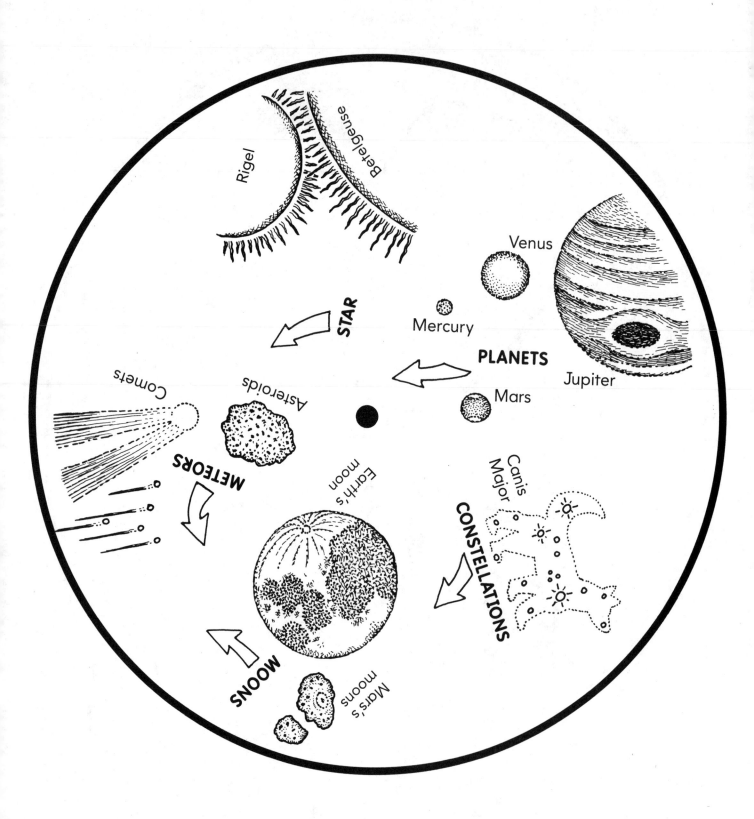

The Water Cycle

Follow water as it moves from the oceans, to the air, to the land, and back again.

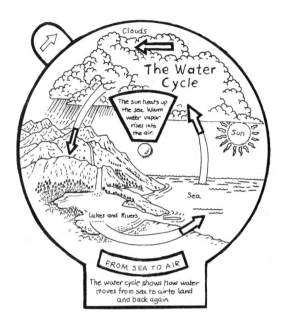

Science Corner

More than 97 percent of the earth's water is salty seawater. With the sun's energy warming up the ocean surface, millions of gallons of seawater *evaporates*—changes from liquid into gas called *water vapor*—every day. Water evaporates from rivers, lakes, streams, and ponds on land as well. Water vapor is also given off when animals breathe out and when plant leaves transpire.

Water vapor rises along with the warm air. The higher warm air rises, the cooler the temperature becomes. Cooler air can't hold as much water vapor as warm air can. At the temperature called the *dew point*, water vapor changes into tiny water droplets. This process of changing from gas into liquid is called *condensation*.

Billions of tiny water droplets group together to form clouds. Winds blow clouds over the ocean and over land. As the air temperature continues to cool down, the tiny droplets in clouds combine to form larger and larger droplets that eventually fall on earth as *precipitation*, usually in the form of rain. Rain falls back in the ocean or on land, depending on where clouds are. At very cold temperatures, water droplets in the air form solid ice crystals that fall as snow. The process of changing from a liquid into a solid is called *freezing*.

During a rainstorm, some water soaks into the soil but most runs off the land into rivers to be carried back to the sea. Snow melts in the warm sun and turns back into liquid water. Every day, rivers return millions of gallons of water back to the ocean. All the ways in which water moves from the sea to the air to the land and back to the sea make up the *water cycle*. Because of the water cycle, water is constantly reused by all living things. Without water there would be no life on earth. Plants and animals must have water to grow, survive, and reproduce.

Materials

* reproducible pages 65 and 66

* scissors

* paper fastener

* colored pencils, crayons, or markers (optional)

More To Do

Don't Forget Snow

Snow is another form of precipitation that plays an important part in the water cycle. Have students find out how snowflakes form in clouds, what happens to snow when it falls to earth, and what happens when it melts. Challenge them to make their own water cycle wheels, replacing rain with snow.

Resources

***The Snowflake: A Water Cycle Story* by Neil Waldman (Milbrook Press, 2003)**

This charming book traces what happens to one droplet of water over an entire year, starting as a snowflake in January.

***The Magic School Bus Wet All Over: A Book About the Water Cycle* by Pat Relf (Scholastic, 1996).**

After evaporating into the air, Ms. Frizzle's class condenses to form a cloud, then rains back down as they take a trip through the water cycle.

http://www.epa.gov/ ogwdw/kids/flash/flash_ watercycle.html

Click on any of the four menu items to set the water cycle in motion.

Making the Wheel

1 Photocopy pages 65 and 66.

2 Cut out THE WATER CYCLE circle and the wheel along the thick outer lines.

3 Cut open the arrows and the CUT OUT windows on the outer circle along the thick solid lines.

4 Place THE WATER CYCLE circle on top of the wheel. Push the paper fastener through the centers of both pieces to join them, as shown.

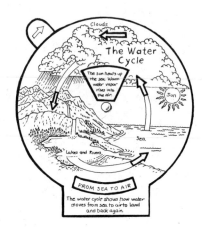

Teaching With the Wheel

Prompt students to think about how they and their families use water in their daily lives. Ask: *Where does the water you use come from? Why do you think that the supply of water never runs out except during a severe drought?*

To learn more about the water cycle, invite students to color, assemble, and read their wheels. Have them turn the wheel clockwise. Then check for understanding by asking them these questions:

1 What is the water cycle? (*The water cycle shows how water moves from sea to air to land and back again.*)

2 How does water get into the air? (*The sun warms up the sea and warm water vapor rises into the air.*)

3 What happens to rain that falls? (*It runs off the land into rivers and back to the sea.*)

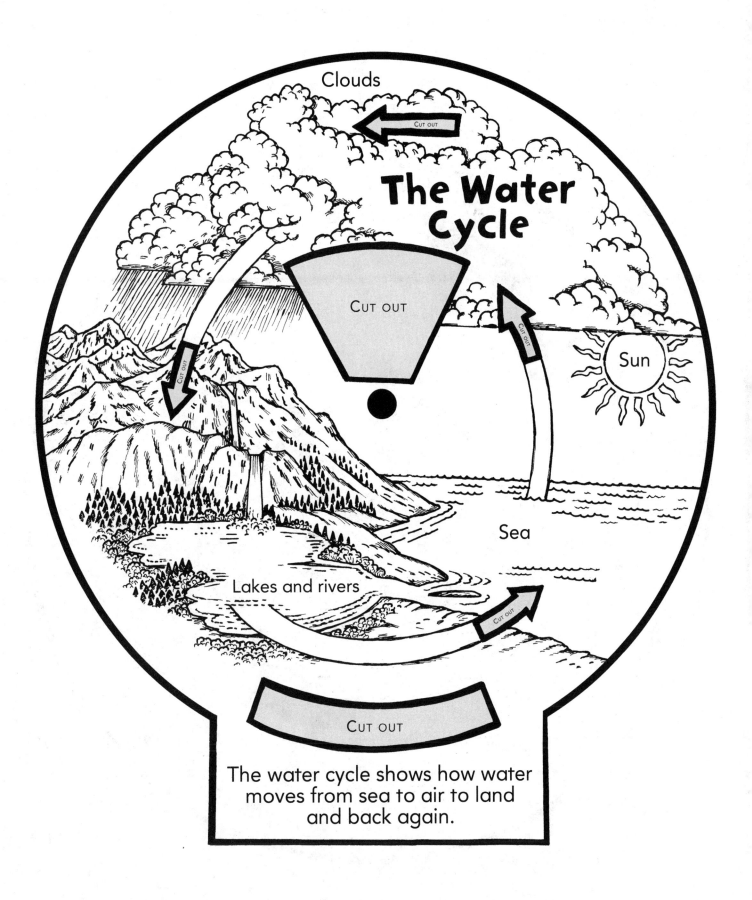

Clouds

The Water Cycle

Cut out

Cut out

Cut out

Sun

Sea

Lakes and rivers

Cut out

Cut out

The water cycle shows how water moves from sea to air to land and back again.

The Water Cycle

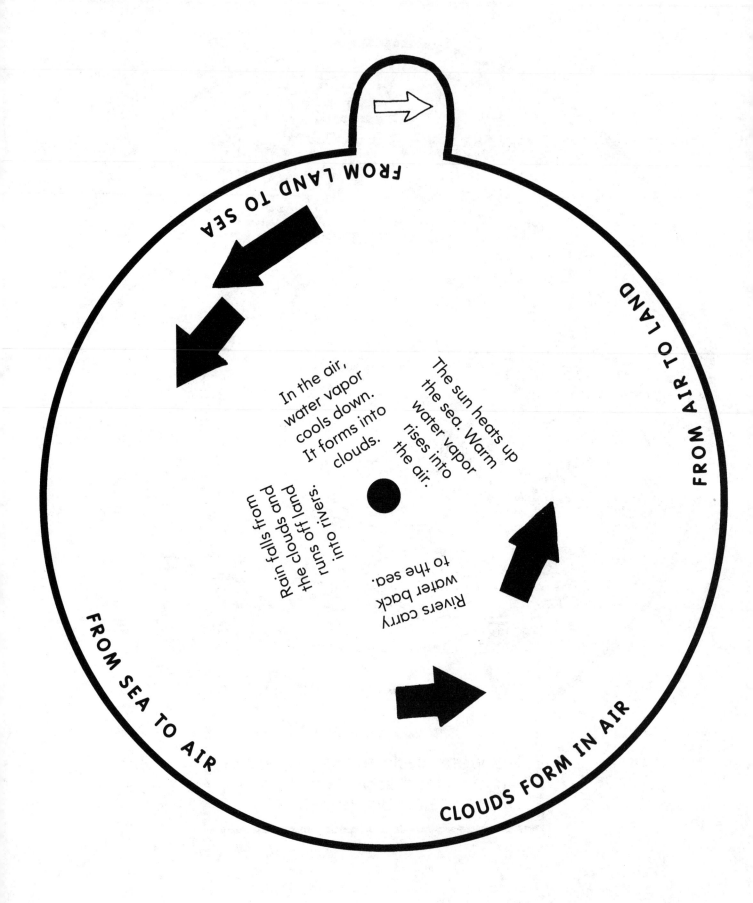

FROM LAND TO SEA

FROM AIR TO LAND

In the air, water vapor cools down. It forms into clouds.

The sun heats up the sea. Warm water vapor rises into the air.

Rain falls from the clouds and runs off land into rivers.

Rivers carry water back to the sea.

FROM SEA TO AIR

CLOUDS FORM IN AIR

What Cloud Is It?

Identify different kinds of clouds and discover where to find them.

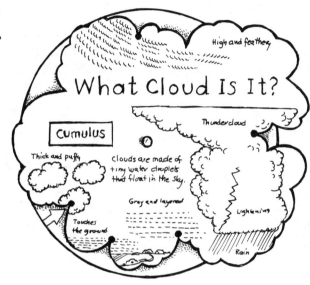

Science Corner

Clouds are made up of billions of tiny water droplets or ice crystals that float in the air. Water in air is often in the form of an invisible gas called *water vapor*. When air temperature cools down enough, water vapor condenses, or changes from a gas into tiny liquid water droplets that gather together to form clouds. As the air gets colder, more droplets join together, get larger and heavier, and eventually fall as rain or snow from the clouds.

Clouds come in different sizes and shapes. Some form high in the sky, while others lay closer to the ground. Students may be surprised to learn that on a foggy day they are actually walking through a cloud—fog is simply a cloud that touches the ground.

The three main kinds of clouds are cirrus, cumulus, and stratus. High, feathery cirrus clouds can signal a change in weather, while thick, puffy cumulus clouds usually bring fair weather. Gray layers of stratus clouds that form low in the sky may block out the sun and produce drizzle. Thick layers of dark stratus clouds usually bring rain or snow. Thunder, lightning, and heavy rain often come from cumulonimbus, or thunderclouds, that pile up high in the sky.

Materials

* reproducible pages 69 and 70
* scissors
* paper fastener
* colored pencils, crayons, or markers (optional)

More To Do

Name That Cloud

Invite students to look out the window and observe clouds at different times of the day. Each time they look have them use their wheels to figure out what kinds of clouds they see in the sky. Have them take their wheels home and figure out what clouds they see over the weekend, draw a picture of the clouds, and label them.

Resources

Clouds by Anne Rockwell (Collins, 2008)

Folk art-style paintings depict different kinds of clouds, while simple text describes each type of cloud, where it forms in the sky, and what kind of weather it brings.

The Kids' Book of Clouds & Sky by Frank Staub (Sterling, 2005)

This question-and-answer book includes excellent photos and kid-friendly text, plus fun weather experiments.

http://www.weatherwizkids .com/weather-clouds.htm

Designed by meteorologist Crystal Wicker, this website answers questions about clouds, including how they form, where to find them, and what they look like.

Making the Wheel

1 Photocopy pages 69 and 70. Color, if desired.

2 Cut out the cloud and the wheel along the thick outer lines.

3 Cut open the CUT OUT window on the cloud along the thick solid lines.

4 Place the cloud on top of the wheel. Push the paper fastener through the centers of both pieces to join them, as shown.

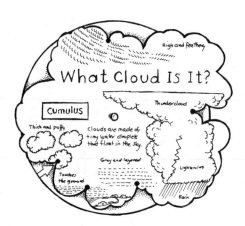

Teaching With the Wheel

Invite students to color, assemble, and read their wheels. To use the wheel, have students turn the circle clockwise until the name of a cloud appears in the window. Then tell them to look for a black arrow pointing to one of the black dots on the cloud piece. The black dot indicates the type of cloud that matches the name in the window. Check for students' understanding by asking them these questions:

1 What is a cloud made of? (*Billions of tiny water droplets that float in the sky*)

2 Which type of cloud brings rain and lightning? (*Cumulonimbus*)

3 Which cloud touches the ground? (*Fog*)

What Cloud Is It?

High and feathery

Thundercloud

Lightning

Rain

Clouds are made of tiny water droplets that float in the sky.

Gray and layered

CUT OUT

Thick and puffy

Touches the ground

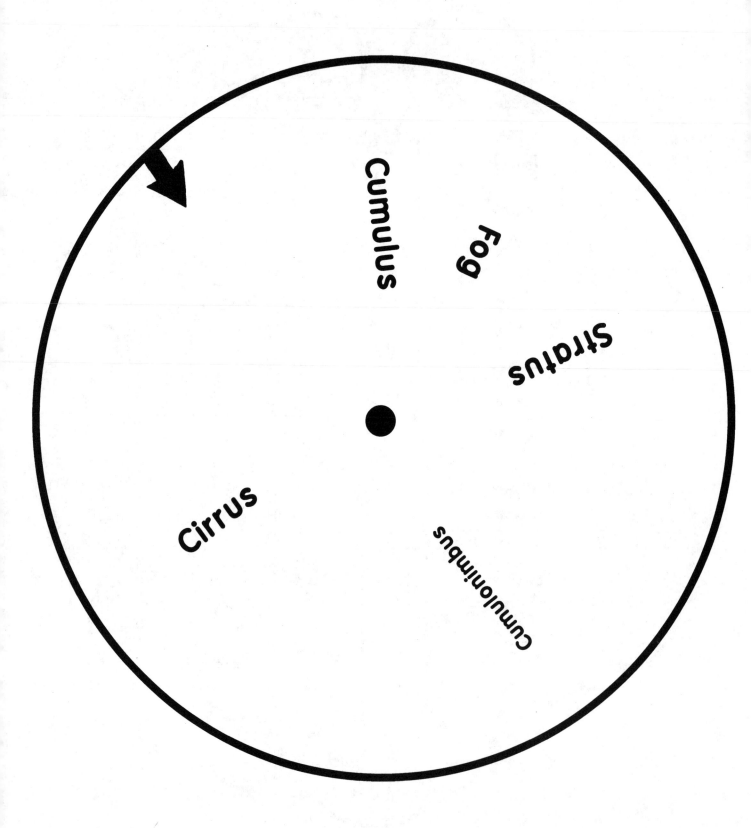

The Seasons and Weather

Students learn how seasons and weather go hand-in-hand with this double wheel.

Science Corner

The Earth is tilted about 23.5 degrees on its axis. As Earth revolves around the sun once every 365.25 days, half of the globe is tilted toward the sun, while the other half is tilted away. Places in Earth's middle to high latitudes experience four seasons because these are where the greatest changes in sunlight and temperature occur.

When it is summer in the Northern Hemisphere, the northern part of the Earth is tilted toward the sun and the sun's energy rays strike the area more directly than they do in winter. In winter, the Northern Hemisphere is tilted away from the sun and the sun's energy rays spread out over a greater area of land on the Earth's curved surface. Such spreading reduces how much energy from the sun the land and water can absorb in winter. As a result, the air is colder in winter than in summer.

During winter, days are shorter and nights longer; in summer, we see the reverse. At the start of autumn and spring, the Earth is neither tilted toward or away from the sun. There are about 12 hours of daylight and 12 hours of night. Depending on where you live, winters may be cold with snow falling and ice forming, or they may be mild and warm. In spring, days get longer and nights get shorter. Temperatures are warmer than in winter, but not as hot as in summer. In most places, it often rains in spring. Flowers bloom and trees grow leaves. Summer days are long and hot, while nights are short and warm. Some places experience rain throughout the summer, while other places see hardly any rain. In autumn, the nights get longer, while the days get shorter. It is cooler than in summer, but not as cold as in winter.

Materials

- reproducible pages 73 and 74
- scissors
- 2 paper fasteners
- colored pencils, crayons, or markers (optional)

More To Do

Weather Report

Select the start of a season during the school year: September 21, December 21, March 21. Over the period of a month have students keep a daily record of the time when the sun rises and sets; the high and low temperatures; and the kind of weather that takes place (windy, snowy, rainy, etc.). Make a chart, and at the end of the month, ask students to describe any trends they see; for example, the days are getting longer or shorter, the temperatures are getting warmer or colder, and so on.

Resources

***Sunshine Makes the Seasons*
by Franklyn M. Branley
(Collins, 2005)**

This easy-to-read, colorful book explains how the sun plays a role in changing of the seasons.

***Seasons of the Year*
by Margaret Hall
(Capstone Press, 2008)**

Text, photographs, and diagrams work together to describe how the seasons are a pattern of nature that keeps recurring.

http://www.youtube.com/ watch?v=LTXtSGfiVdY

Invite young students to sing along with this music video that describes the four seasons.

Making the Wheel

1 Photocopy pages 73 and 74. Color, if desired.

2 Cut out the three pieces along the thick outer lines.

3 Place the SEASONS wheel under the top of the big piece. Push a paper fastener through the black dots to join them, as shown.

4 Place the WEATHER wheel under the bottom of the big piece. Push a paper fastener though the black dots to join them.

Teaching With the Wheel

Introduce the wheel to students by asking them: *What season are we in? What has the weather been like? How do you think the weather will change next season?*

To learn more about seasons and the weather, invite students to color, assemble, and read their wheels. To use, have them turn the top wheel to a season, then turn the bottom wheel to the kind of weather they think will occur in their city or town during that season. Then check for understanding by asking them these questions:

1 What are the four seasons? (*Winter, spring, summer, autumn*)

2 In which season are days long and nights short? (*Summer*)

3 What kind of weather can take place during the winter? (*Answers will vary, depending on your location. It can be sunny, rainy, windy, or snowy.*)

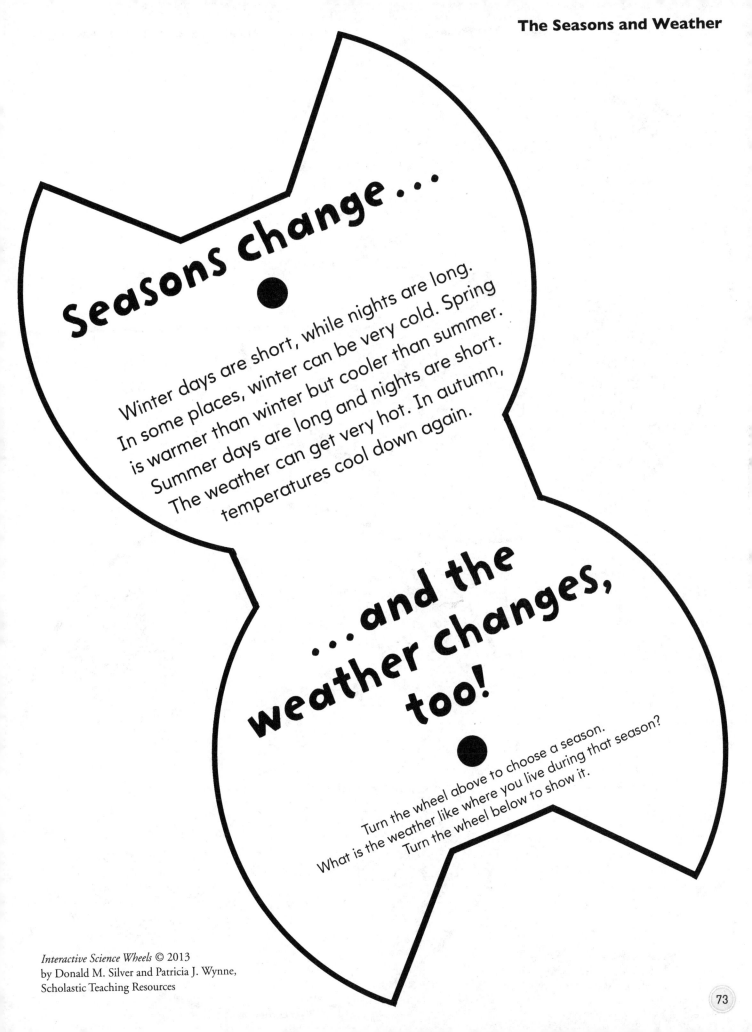

Seasons change...

Winter days are short, while nights are long. In some places, winter can be very cold. Spring is warmer than winter but cooler than summer. Summer days are long and nights are short. The weather can get very hot. In autumn, temperatures cool down again.

...and the weather changes, too!

Turn the wheel above to choose a season. What is the weather like where you live during that season? Turn the wheel below to show it.

Interactive Science Wheels © 2013 by Donald M. Silver and Patricia J. Wynne, Scholastic Teaching Resources

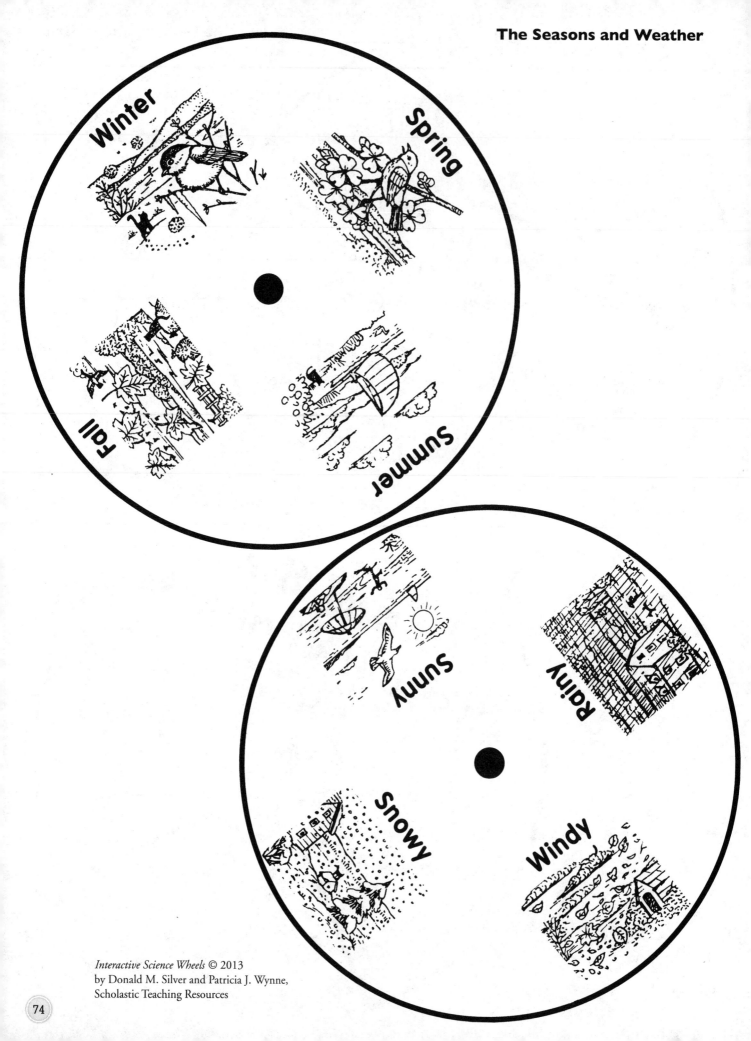

Interactive Science Wheels © 2013
by Donald M. Silver and Patricia J. Wynne,
Scholastic Teaching Resources

What Are Simple Machines?

Explore four different kinds of simple machines to find out what they do.

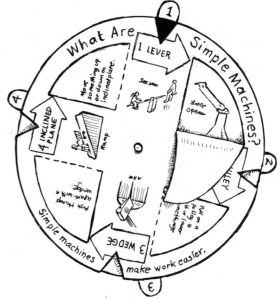

Science Corner

Simple machines are tools that enable people to do work. For scientists, *work* means moving an object a certain distance. It takes *force* to move an object. A force is a push or a pull. When the force of the wind pushes the sails on a sailboat, the boat moves. When you throw a ball up in the air, the force of gravity pulls it down.

When people use simple machines to do work, the machines don't change how much work is done. But they make the work easier for people to do. Some simple machines reduce the amount of force needed to move an object; some change the direction in which the force has to be applied; and some do both. There are six simple machines—the lever, the inclined plane, the pulley, the wedge, the wheel and axle, and the screw. (Only four are shown on the wheel.)

A *lever*, such as a seesaw, is a bar or a board that rests on a turning point called a *fulcrum*. A lever's (or any machine's) *load* is the object that it moves. An *inclined plane*, such as a ramp, is a flat surface that is higher at one end. A *pulley*, such as on a flagpole, is made up of a rope and a wheel. The rope fits onto a groove in the wheel, and the load is attached to one end of the rope. By pulling on the free end of the rope, the wheel moves and the load is raised, lowered, or moved sideways. A *wedge*, such as an axe, is made up of two inclined planes joined together. The ends of the inclined planes meet to form a sharp edge that can push things, such as wood, apart.

Materials

* reproducible pages 77 and 78

* scissors

* paper fastener

* colored pencils, crayons, or markers (optional)

More To Do

Simple Search

Take the class on a walk around the school in search of simple machines. Have students look for inclined planes (ramps, ladders), levers (door hinges, faucets), pulleys (flagpole), and wedges (doorstops, forks). When they find something that they think is a simple machine, have them draw it, explain what kind of machine it is, and record where they found it.

Resources

Simple Machines by Allan Fowler (Children's Press, 2001)

This introductory book describes simple machines and shows how people use them.

Forces Make Things Move by Kimberly Brubaker Bradley (Collins, 2005)

Colorful illustrations combined with simple text help students understand why forces must be applied to make simple machines work.

http://www.edheads.org/ activities/simple-machines/ index.shtml

Set kids on a scavenger hunt to search for simple machines around this virtual house. To access the game, click on Start, then on The House.

Making the Wheel

1 Photocopy pages 77 and 78. Color, if desired.

2 Cut out the two pieces along the thick outer lines.

3 On the WHAT ARE SIMPLE MACHINES? piece, cut open the windows and the four triangular notches along the thick solid lines. For each window, make sure you cut two sides only; do not cut the dashed fold lines.

4 Place the circle with windows on top of the wheel with the tabs. Push the paper fastener through the centers of both pieces to join them, as shown.

Teaching With the Wheel

Invite students to color, assemble, and read their wheels. Have them turn the tabs until number 1 on the tab matches number 1 on the top circle. Have students read about levers, then open the window to find another example of a lever. Repeat for tabs 2, 3, and 4. Then check for understanding by asking students these questions:

1 What do simple machines do? (*Simple machines make work easier.*)

2 Name four kinds of simple machines. (*Lever, inclined plane, wedge, and pulley*)

3 Explain what each machine is used for. (*A lever is used to lift, lower, or move something. An inclined plane is used to move something up or down. A wedge is used to push things apart. A pulley is used to lift or lower something.*)

4 Name an example of each kind of machine. (*Answers will vary.*)

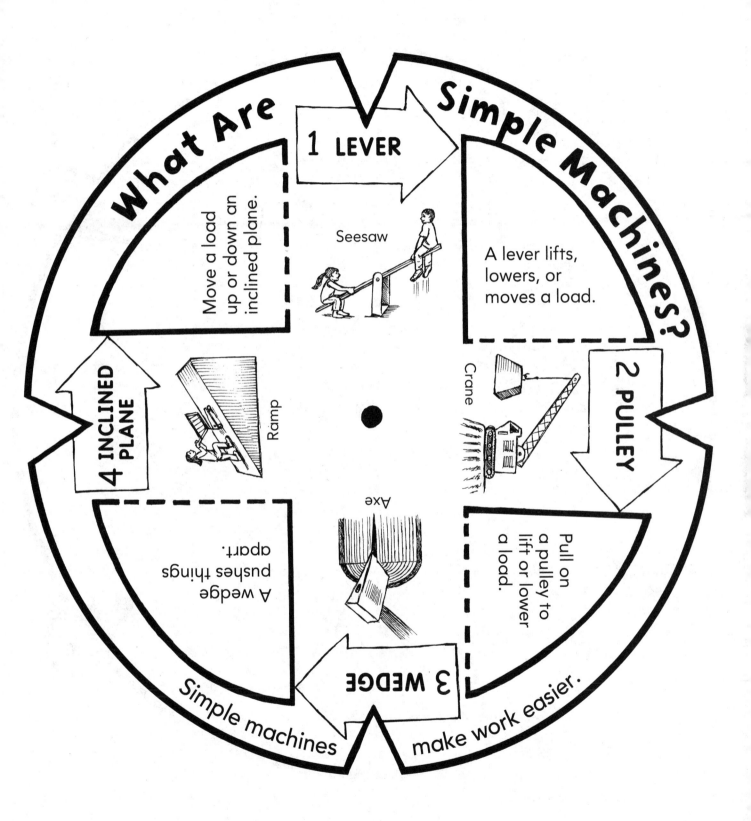

What Are Simple Machines?

1 LEVER

Seesaw

A lever lifts, lowers, or moves a load.

Move a load up or down an inclined plane.

4 INCLINED PLANE

Ramp

Crane

2 PULLEY

Pull on a pulley to lift or lower a load.

Axe

A wedge pushes things apart.

3 WEDGE

Simple machines make work easier.

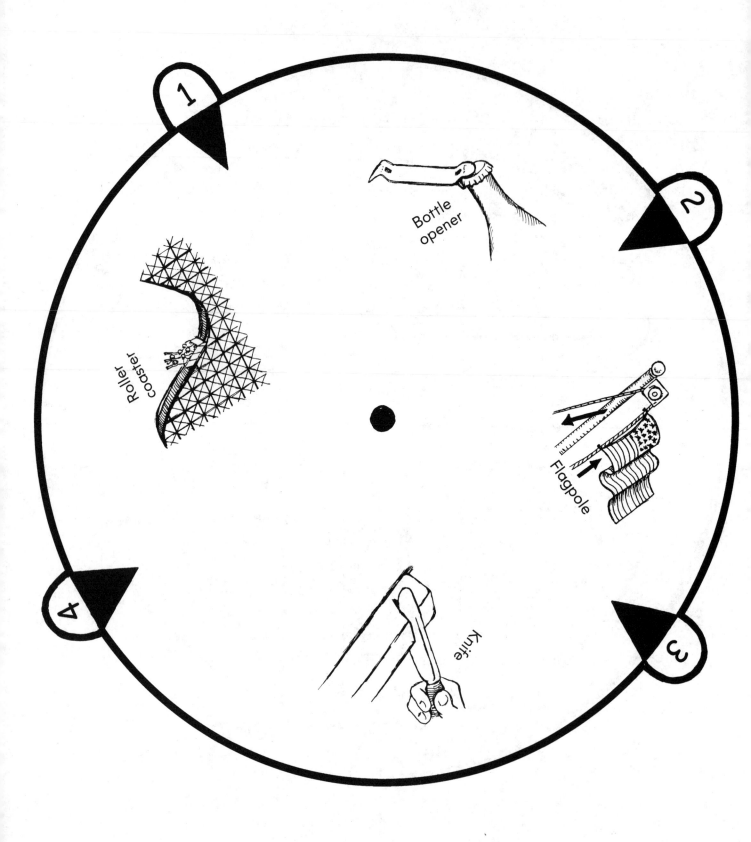

Bottle opener

Roller coaster

Flagpole

Knife

Notes

Notes